Away To Me, Me, My Love

A Sheepdog's Tale of Two Lives

NAOMI MCDONALD

BALBOA.
PRESS
A DIVISION OF HAY HOUSE

Balboa Press books may be ordered through booksellers or by contacting:

Balboa Press
A Division of Hay House
1663 Liberty Drive
Bloomington, IN 47403
www.balboapress.com
1 (877) 407-4847

Print information available on the last page.

ISBN: 978-1-9822-3105-7 (sc)
ISBN: 978-1-9822-3104-0 (hc)
ISBN: 978-1-9822-3152-1 (e)

Library of Congress Control Number: 2019909815

Balboa Press rev. date: 09/10/2019

Foreword

M any believe that each animal that comes into our lives brings a special gift and is with us for a unique purpose. Whether that be to serve as a companion dog for many years or to pass briefly through one's life to reawaken joy, each purpose is as valuable as the next.

But sometimes there are those animals who come to us to help broaden our spiritual horizons and to remember who we are and what we came to do in this lifetime.

Such is the case with Luke and Naomi. Karmic recognition, remembering past lives, and fulfilling compelling dreams weave together to create this magical true story of a woman and her dog who help each other overcome their greatest self-doubts and fears on what is clearly a predestined journey that they can only make together.

I have known Naomi for many years and have been privileged to work with her in animal communication, teach at her ranch, and... to meet her precious Luke. I was thrilled when she asked me to read her manuscript and am honored to offer this Foreword. The memoir is a unique form of literature that, when well done, not only lays out a story but lays bare and exposes the author's very being. This memoir does exactly that, as the beauty and pathos of Luke and Naomi's story reflects themes of the author's entire life and how, as steel is forged through fire, Naomi's character was shaped and strengthened by the abuse she suffered as a child.

Away to Me, My Love is galvanizing, heartwarming, and heart-wrenching, as well as incredibly entertaining with its fascinating descriptions of the sheepherding world and its trials and tribulations.

Everyone who loves animals, and anyone who has partnered with one on the spiritual journey toward self-realization, will be entranced by this special memoir.

Leta Worthington
www.herbsandanimals.com
Learn How to Talk to Animals: A Practical Guide for a Magical Journey
Animal Afterlife: In Their Own Words

Introduction

It was never my intention to be a storyteller. The original purpose of this diary was to revisit a profound journey with my friend, my partner, my loved one—a Border Collie named Luke.

When Luke came into our family as a nine-month-old puppy, his only purpose was to fulfill my twenty-year dream of competing in sheepherding trials. Little did I know how much he would change not only the entire course of my life but the lives of many others as well.

As the words came to life on these pages, I realized my journey with my beloved—now departed—companion was far from over. The most important element of our relationship was yet to come, the telling of our story. During the writing process with my good friend Rhonda, she suggested I include events from my childhood. My response, "No, that's not necessary," came so quickly, she suffered from word-lash.

At a crucial point in Luke's and my years together, a blessing shrouded in a six-foot-tall expression of hate appeared in my world. Demeaning opinions and comments expressed by a person of authority pierced my soul like a hammer: cold, hard, and unrelenting. I found myself making a decision that would throw me into an abyss of sadness so deep that I could see no way out.

It was during this time of wallowing in self-recrimination that I was guided to a place I thought existed only in fairy tales, a place of shamans, a place of spiritual connections, a place of magical healing.

Two things happened as I wrote the stories of Luke's and my time together. First, the long-ago memories returned swift and clear, as if I were experiencing the events and emotions all over again. Second, I could sense his spirit beside me, encouraging me, urging me to continue when the writing seemed too difficult, too painful, or too overwhelming.

As the manuscript came to what I thought was the end, a realization swept through my heart and mind with the power of a tidal wave. Rhonda had been right. For me to understand the woman I have become, I had to understand the events that formed me. Truly knowing myself was not a goal but a road that had two branches: this lifetime and past lifetimes. While traveling along these branches I came to understand that the most ordinary of women could find herself on an extraordinary path of self-discovery and growth.

Armed with Luke's spiritual protective presence, I took the plunge into childhood memories—memories so traumatic that I found small pieces of my soul had splintered away into a realm of safety, to return only when my mind and heart had been healed enough to offer a safe haven.

As I relived these memories from a place of nonjudgment, I could break the old threads of toxic emotions. I could erase the old tapes of unworthiness that cycled through my mind. I could embrace the gifts that had been buried within each childhood memory, the gifts of strength, forgiveness, and tenacity. Letting go of my victim identity allowed the youthful parts of my soul to bound joyfully into my life once more, allowing me to reach the part of myself that saw more beauty in the world. I saw that sharing our story would help others do the same.

It all began with a black-and-white Border Collie and the desire to work sheep.

Chapter One

"Pleeease," begged my friend Ellie Bennett. "I don't want to walk through the fair by myself. Come on. At least watch the sheepherding with me. My neighbor's dog is competing."

With the phone pressed between my ear and shoulder, I shook my head. My aunt Evelyn had planned an outing with my daughter, Heather. Finally, I had a day alone, and the last thing I wanted to do was sit on metal bleachers in a smelly arena watching dogs run around.

"Please," Ellie repeated. "I'll buy you all the junky fair food you can eat. I'll help you feed your horse. I'll clean his stall. Please!"

I rubbed my forehead as if I could will an excuse to pop into my mind. Finally, I sighed.

"I know, I know!" Ellie burst out. "The next time that guy from work asks you out, I'll watch Heather." She chuckled mischievously. "All night, if you want me to."

"Gemini, Ellie." I blushed, feeling my ears turn hot. "I'm not looking for that kind of relationship!" However, I couldn't deny that a movie and dinner would be nice. Besides, all she wanted was just a couple of hours at the fair. What could it hurt?

I groaned. "Fine."

"Great! I'll pick you up in thirty minutes."

An hour later, we were at the fair, looking at the timing sheets for the dogs. "There must be a hundred dogs here," Ellie said, her voice pitched high. "Buster doesn't run until late this afternoon."

I repressed an exasperated sigh. *Oh, good. An entire day of hard bleachers and sweat.*

Lying on blankets or in crates, tethered dogs lined one wall behind the bleachers. To my surprise, none of them barked.

I took in a deep breath and smiled. The freshly turned arena soil emitted a rich, earthy smell. Men and women of all ages prepared to compete with their dogs. The air held electric anticipation.

A short, stocky female handler walked into the arena with a slick-coated black-and-white Border Collie. She held a carved wooden crook in her left hand. Her dog sat on her right.

The woman said, "Away to me," and the dog ran up the fence line.

Instantly, I felt propelled to the edge of my seat. My entire world consisted of a dog, four sheep, and the sound of a whistle.

As the day progressed, I found that Border Collies were the predominate breed in the event, but there were also Belgian sheepdogs, Corgis, and Australian shepherds. With an inherent instinct and style all their own, Border Collies had the stealth and fluid movement of a predator cat and the quick side-to-side reflexes of a cutting horse.

"He came around too far," I shouted as a smallish red-and-white dog with a rough coat ran around a sheep all the way to its ear, turning all four critters too sharply so they missed an obstacle. My voice grew raspy like a rabid fan at a football game.

Some people say the definition of magic is "making things happen through intention." If that's true, this was magic. At a command, the dogs would move up, down, left, right, slow, fast.

As expected, the sheep moved when the dog did. However, some dogs could maneuver the sheep simply by staring at them.

Everything about the dogs—their body language, their eagerness to work, their obedience to commands—said, *I'm doing what I was born to do.*

A sharp, high-pitched laugh brought me back to earth.

"I had to barter my life away to get you here," Ellie said as her laughing ceased. "You're sure wound up now."

"I am, I guess." I chuckled. "I don't know. It's like I've been here before... like I know these dogs, like I have a kinship with them or something."

My friend grew serious. "Maybe in another lifetime you were a sheep or a shepherd."

I went to elbow her, but another dog came in the arena, and I forgot everything else.

Ellie's comment tickled at something, though. Whenever I closed my eyes, the sound of the handler's whistle brought images of distant mountains, green rolling hills, and a black-and-white dog.

I shivered despite the heat of the day. "I don't know if I believe in multiple lifetimes," I said, "but I do know one thing. I'm going to have a herding dog one day."

Chapter Two

MANY YEARS LATER

The twilight glow lit the evening in a tapestry of pinks, blues, and golds. I rode my horse, Wynona Belle, around the end of the arena at a slow canter. As we approached the long side, her speed gradually increased until I felt as if she were gliding above the ground. When her back rounded under my saddle to take an elongated stride, I relaxed my spine, pushed down in the stirrups, lowered the bridle reins slightly and in almost a whisper said, "Whoa."

The mare planted both hind feet equally on the arena surface. As she walked on her front legs, her back ones left two parallel fifteen-foot slide marks in the perfectly groomed sandy loam.

"Good girl." I stroked the neck of my chestnut-colored mare. Wynonna Belle's sides were heaving with exertion. As she stood in the still air, sweat streamed from under her saddle. Even though I hadn't stepped up into a stirrup until eight o'clock, we were enduring the sweltering heat of an Oklahoma summer.

In another moment, Stan Abernathy, doctor of veterinary medicine, rode up beside me and executed the same maneuver. Tall and lean, he patted his horse and nodded at me. "You outdid us. Her slide marks are longer every time you bring her."

"Thanks," I said. "I don't have outdoor arena lights at Dream

Maker Ranch, so I ride customer horses when it's cool in the mornings. Coming here and riding under your lights at night allows me to spend more time on my own horse."

"Glad to have the company," Stan said, his handlebar moustache twitching. Long graying sideburns sprouted like toothbrushes from under his straw cowboy hat.

I gazed at the long tracks behind me. "That," I said, "is a good place to stop for the evening."

As we rode around the arena at a slow walk, the caterwauling of a litter of coyote pups echoed through the still night air.

"Those pups are really close," I said. "I would have thought you were too urban for them to live here."

A small white dog dashed through the arena toward the sound. Stan shouted, "Peggy Sue, leave it. Come on, get over here."

Within seconds, a Jack Russell Terrier ran under the fence and jumped into a chair that sat by the barn.

First year we've had the noisy bastards. They drive Peggy Sue crazy. She doesn't know that Momma Coyote would serve her up as a puppy meal."

As we rode by Peggy Sue's chair, I said, "Peggy Sue's cute, but you don't strike me as a Jack Russell kind of guy."

"Aw, I inherited the little hard-headed sprout from the man that I partner with on this stud." Stan reached down and stroked the flaxen mane of Baylor, a sorrel quarter horse. The gentleness of the gesture contrasted to the appearance of the grizzled veterinarian. The evident admiration he had for the horse shone through his eyes.

As we walked, the sun disappeared. Floodlights illuminated the area inside the fence and blacked out the stars. The total darkness that surrounded the arena gave a feeling that we were the only beings in existence—at least until another blast of coyote caterwauling rang out. This one was followed shortly by growls and snarls. Chills ran up my spine. Wynona's body tensed, her ears perked up, and she glanced into the darkness.

Stan stroked Baylor again as if to settle him, then glanced over at Peggy Sue. "You stay right where you are, little lady," he growled.

I felt my eyebrows rise as the dog hunkered down in the chair. "She knows your tone, that's for sure."

Normally, after a long day an irresistible pull toward my shower and bed would override any desire to ride around and chat. As soon as Wynonna Belle cooled down, we would be on our way home. But that night, I wasn't in a hurry to go out in the blackness where my trailer was parked.

"You mentioned Peggy Sue came from your partner. Why do you have a partner?"

"I only have five acres here. Charlie Cameron, my partner, has a large ranch in Arkansas. He takes care of the foals we raise until they're two years old. Then, I start them. Most we sell. This guy, though." He patted Baylor. "This guy's a keeper."

I nodded.

"Charlie raises Jacks and Border Collies," Stan went on. "Peggy Sue was a runt. He couldn't sell her, so I took her. Most days, I don't want to shoot her." He made a sound that could have been a cough or a chuckle.

My eyes grew round, as I wasn't quite sure if he was serious or joking. I asked, "Border Collies... Does Charlie do herding? I went to a sheep trial years ago and loved it."

"Yep, he's got some of the best pedigrees around. He imported a bitch and stud dog from Scotland several years ago."

A sudden pang went through my chest, and my heart lurched. Why was I having such a physical and emotional reaction to a simple statement about dogs? To hide my rising fears, I suddenly had to rearrange the angle that Wynonna's bridle reins lay on her neck. Was I reacting to Stan's mention of herding dogs?

When I couldn't avert my eyes or blink away the dampness any longer, I said, "I think she's cooled enough." I felt relieved to find an excuse to ride away. At the trailer, my hands shook slightly as I loosened the cinch that held Wynonna's saddle. Was it the eerie coyote sounds and the darkness that set my emotions on edge? I shook my head.

I had to get a grip. Stan didn't need to think he was riding with an overemotional, crying, crazy woman.

By the time I got back to Stan for a quick goodbye, he had exchanged Baylor's bridle for a nylon halter, tied him to the pipe fence, and unsaddled him. "Your mare's got talent. Keep doing what you're doing," he said. "When it's this hot, I ride most every night. The gate's always open."

"Thank you." I nodded. "I'll see you on Tuesday."

Once home, I washed off Wynonna's sweat, bedded her down in her stall, and gave her hay. As I lay down next to my husband, Mac, my thoughts stayed at full tilt. Dogs and sheep and my friend Ellie danced their way through my mind until the wee hours.

Chapter Three

I couldn't be sure when I'd fallen asleep, but the next thing I knew, Mac wrenched open the window blinds, filling the room with the first rays of sun.

"You said to get you up at five-thirty," he said. "I'm leaving for work soon. Get a move on, woman."

"You woke me up from the best dream," I complained. "I was reliving the first time I saw a herding competition." I stretched and got to my feet. "I remembered everything. I could even smell the freshly worked dirt. I loved it, Mac. The dogs were wonderful. I vowed I would have a herding dog and work sheep someday."

Mac's sky-blue eyes wrinkled in the corners. "What brought that on? The last thing you need is something else to take up your time."

"While we were cooling the horses down, Stan mentioned that a friend of his raised Border Collies and I guess it triggered something… really triggered something. I still feel shaky."

I followed Mac to the kitchen and made two cups of coffee, one in a to-go cup and one in a ceramic cup for me. "I felt so silly," I concluded. "Who gets that worked up about the thought of owning a dog?"

While Mac slid papers into his brown leather briefcase, he said, "Maybe you'll have a herding dog one day when you're not so busy. When life settles down, you can do some research, find a nice trained dog, and take some lessons, just like buying a horse." He turned to me with his signature huge, toothy smile.

Instantly, my heart flew up to my throat. Something I loathed to do was compare Mac to my former husband, my daughter Heather's father. In this case, I couldn't help myself. Instead of telling me how ridiculous I was for becoming emotional for no apparent reason, he gave me credit, knowing I would work through it. Instead of telling me I had no business starting a new project, he gave me hope for the future.

Mac's full lower lip turned down. "What's up? You're looking at me funny."

My mind froze under a wave of the mighty what-if's. What if I had turned away from this man when he eased his way into our lives? What if I had let the fear of repeating my mother's mistakes send me running in the opposite direction?

I forced a smile. "Oh, I just appreciate you, is all." Then, the smile took over. "And... you are kinda cute." I raised my eyebrows up and down.

"Is that a pickup brow?" He picked me up by the waist and swung me around, my head near the ceiling.

I giggled and kissed the top of his blond head. "Okay, Hercules, you'd better get to work."

Chapter Four

"Hi, I'm Charlie Cameron," said a deep, melodic baritone voice on the other end of the barn phone. "Stan Abernathy suggested I give you a call."

I had ridden with Stan a few more times, and, to my great relief, the topic of dogs had not come up again. It took a few moments to collect my thoughts. *Why would Stan's partner call me?*

His rich voice made me want to listen to anything he said. If he'd recited cookbook recipes, I might have taken up baking. "Oh, I remember," I said. "You're partners with him on that gorgeous stud."

"Baylor, yeah. They don't come along that nice very often. I keep getting good reports from Stan on his progress."

"I bet." I paused, knowing he didn't call me to discuss his horse.

"Stan mentioned you're interested in herding. My wife's been sick, and I have two Border Collie pups I haven't had time for. He thought you might want to take a look."

My pulse quickened for only an instant, but then a calm reserve came over me. *I'm over it,* I told myself.

To Charlie, I said, "It was nice of you to call, but I have more than I can handle with my horse business. I can't take on another project. I do want a herding dog someday, but I'm after a trained Border Collie to learn with. When the time is right, I'll call you or let him know."

"I hear ya. Between my wife, all the horses around here, and this farm, the dogs have taken a backseat. These two males have pretty much been left in kennels. I've never had to do that before. Can I give you some information in case you hear of anyone who might want a nice pup?"

"Sure." I let out a silent sigh. I had managed to tell him no without shaking or tears. The sudden onslaught of emotion a few weeks ago must have been triggered by that old memory of the fair. Today, I was back to being a sensible businesswoman.

"These dogs are seven months old. I imported both grandparents about five years ago from Scotland. I can fax you copies of their papers if someone's interested. It's been a real successful line in cattle and sheepherding."

As I leaned against the door frame of the barn, listening to that resonate baritone, I watched a hummingbird flitter about and dine on purple salvia.

"So, these two have potential," Charlie went on. "But, unfortunately, they haven't had any handling or training. Rough-coated, handsome boys, both of them. One pup is outgoing and showing signs of being aggressive, which isn't a bad thing in a working dog. The other one is shy, so he'll take some time."

Time... I studied the nearby hummingbird. Hummingbirds didn't think in terms of time. Their journey seemed sacred somehow, divinely driven, without worry or regret.

"Hum." My attention turned back to Charlie. "Does that mean one has more instinct than the other?"

"Not necessarily," he said. "Often, it only means a different herding style. A quiet dog is sometimes a very powerful dog."

Hummingbirds are quiet and powerful. This one took my mind away again. It was as if she had a map imprinted on her spirit that neither time or distance could erase. I shifted the phone to the other ear. Come to think of it, I had witnessed that very thing in the Border Collies I had watched so many years ago—a natural instinct to fulfill some internal need.

My heart did its own little flutter and flew past my brain. Before I could think, I heard myself say, "I want the shy one."

After a pause that lasted an eternity, Charlie asked, "Are you sure? He's the opposite of what you *just* said you wanted... Why don't you let me do some checking and see if I can find at least a started dog for you?"

"No. I want the shy one."

Charlie let out a huff of air. "Okay, I'll start handling him and get him leash trained. I'm going to be coming to Stan's in the next few weeks to watch the stud work, so I'll bring the dog. If you don't want the boy when you see him, you don't have to take him."

My hand shook as I hung up the phone. What in the galloping green gargoyles had I just committed to?

Chapter Five

S oiled shavings and manure flew six feet into the air behind me and landed on the ground as the tractor and spreader passed over the newly sprouted bluestem. I had grown accustomed to the song the machinery sang as I drove—the jingle of the conveyer chain, the clank of the gears, and whirr of the horizontal auger.

A few weeks before, Mac had said, beaming, "Steel is the appropriate medium for an eleven-year anniversary." He was clearly impressed with his own cleverness. "I know it will be put to good use." His blue eyes danced.

That's how my bright green 1949 John Deere manure spreader had become one of my most valued possessions.

A light rain brought up the scent of moist earth. I shivered and pulled the hood of my slicker over my head.

To the rhythm of the jingle, clank, and whirr, I tried to picture the now nine-month-old dog whose arrival I had anticipated for the last two months. Really, now that I thought about it, I had anticipated his arrival somewhere in my heart for the last twenty years. He wouldn't have that cute puppy smell I loved. He'd be gangly and past the fuzzy-ball-of-fur stage. A rough-coated Border Collie had long, silky hair, and I couldn't wait to run my fingers through it. I couldn't wait to begin learning how to train him. After today, he would be a member of our family.

As quickly as the excitement about making the dog part of our family arrived, a very different emotion crept in to take its place. *What if this was a mistake?* How could I have made such a rash decision? I knew how emotionally, financially, and physically damaging an untrained, unproven animal and a new competitor could be to each other.

Then the danged-old what-if's monster attacked me again. What if this dog had no herding instincts? What if he was resistant to training? What if he had physical limitations that would render him unable to do the job? What was I thinking when I made a commitment to an unseen Border Collie from a friend of a friend? Hello, I didn't own a single sheep, let alone know how to care for one or have a safe place to keep one.

The rain subsided. I put the tractor in gear and drove on. The jingle and clank had silenced, telling me the shavings and manure were all broadcast. I jumped down to disengage the spreader gear when a coyote sprang from the grass and ran for the five-acre pond.

"What the heck?" I screeched. My nerves were already close to the surface, and the fright covered my skin with pinpricks.

Droplets of water flew from the tall grass into the air, marking its path. The creature stopped under the huge willow tree that crowned the dam bordering the pond.

"What are you doing out in the day?" I asked. "I only hear you around dusk. Did I drive by your den and scare you? Do you have babies somewhere?"

Our property was much more rural than Stan's, so we had always had a distant coyote population. The bittersweet, high-pitched keening of the pups would tell us they were feeding. Bobbie Jo, our Lhasa Apso, didn't go out at night without one of us with her. On the other hand, Bootsie Myrtle, our barn cat, had been with us for ten years and could outsmart a coyote any day.

Once I quit babbling, I noticed the coyote seemed to be purposefully holding my attention. She was thin. Her brown fur had patches missing along one side. Her black-tipped ears pointed like radar beacons in my direction. Her black eyes appeared too large for her face as she stared intently at me.

Time stood still. My skin no longer prickled. The fearful voice inside me went calm.

A breeze and a sliver of sun shone through the willow, and glittering drops rained down. The coyote shook water in all directions and took off through our neighbor's woods.

I drew in a long breath. "Okay then," I said, and patted the steering wheel of my trusty tractor.

Tattered bands of gray clouds stretched across the sky in front of me. I glanced over my shoulder to see a solid band of darkness promising a downpour. Faraway lightning tore a jagged slash across the ominous clouds.

The coyote forgotten, I rushed to bring the horses in from their turnout pens.

Chapter Six

Just as I led the last horse into her stall, the radio announcer said, "The time is now eleven-thirty a.m. Expect a drop-in temperature as a storm front moves through Green County this afternoon."

"That's for sure," I responded to the unseen voice at K93.5.

Dry leaves and grass spun in a whirlwind just inside the giant sliding barn door. I grabbed the handle with my left hand, braced my arm on the frame, and heaved with all my weight as the wind pushed against it like a powerful fist. After I latched the door, the only remaining sign of Mother Nature's ravings was the debris that now lay on the ground.

I ran the checklist through my mind. The gate to the riding arena in the north end of the barn was closed. The wash stall in the south end was clean. All the horses were munching hay.

A bit worse for wear after morning chores, my T-shirt and jeans were passably clean. In a little while, my friend Peggy would be here, and we could drive to Stan's veterinary clinic in Broken Arrow and pick up my long-awaited herding dog.

"This dog might not be what you want," Charlie had said during our last conversation. "He's still pretty shy. I can take him right back with me. You're under no obligation."

However, from the time I'd uttered the words, "I'll take the shy one," I'd had the feeling that he was mine. The feeling stayed there and got bigger and bigger.

Last night, while I loaded the dishwasher something suddenly clicked while Mac was in the living room, laughing at a comedy on the television.

"His name is Luke," I said, plopping down beside him.

"Hmm?"

"Luke. His name is Luke."

When Mac finally tore his attention away from the movie, he said, "Who, the mailman? Is there something I should know?"

A huff of exasperation escaped my chest. "No, this is serious. My herding dog. He'll be here tomorrow. You know how important this is."

When my husband spoke, his words were clipped and short. "Look, he's a dog—just a dog. How can you name an animal you haven't seen? How can you call him a herding dog when he hasn't been trained? A horse is just a horse until you teach them reining, pleasure, or trail. You're making a lot of assumptions on the word of a man you don't know, about a dog you've never seen."

"Stick out your tongue," I ordered.

"What? No."

"Stick out your tongue," I repeated. "Your attitude is so lemony, it has to be yellow. You don't have to be so tart and thick-skinned. You don't have to divide everything in segments."

Mac pressed his lips together and squinted his eyes.

He looked so silly that all the tension left my body and I chuckled. "Now you look like you've been sucking lemons."

In an instant, Mac's face softened. Kindness hovered behind his words. "You're just not thinking things through like you usually do. You seem to be going blindly into something that's important to you in a way I don't understand. I don't want to see you hurt, that's all."

Today, as I worked, I kept thinking about the previous evening's conversation. Was that the reason for the doubt and panic this morning? Was my husband right?

As I walked by, Wynonna Belle brushed her nose against the bars of her stall. I stopped and stroked the velvet softness. "You're so lovely, Miss Belle, and you're becoming quite the accomplished reining horse. This dog will be the herding dog I've been waiting for," I told her.

As I passed through the tack room, I noticed Bootsie Myrtle, our resident pest control and teaching assistant. "Okay, sleepyhead. Time to go out. I'm locking up." I picked the snoozing gray bobtail cat from a saddle seat. Her white paws gave her the appearance that she was wearing tiny boots.

The song "Boogie Shoes" echoed down the barn aisle from the radio. Bootsie Myrtle lay comfortably in my arms as I danced to the front of the building, singing, "You already have on your, your, your boogie shoes, I'll boogie with you."

"Well, a singing, dancing cat," said a soft voice behind me.

Startled, I turned to see my friend Peggy grinning. "I didn't hear you come in," I replied, blushing.

"I slipped in the small door. It's nasty out there. We'll be driving in the storm."

"Yeah, so will Charlie with my dog. They're coming from Arkansas. Let me take Bobbie Jo in the house." I set Bootsie Myrtle on the ground and picked up my sweet-faced Lhasa Apso.

Peggy laughed. "Her fur is covered in hay."

"There's no help for it now. No one told her she wasn't a barn dog. I don't have time to brush it out. I'll meet you in the truck."

Bobbie Jo and I made the short dash into the laundry room. "I'll be gone a few hours," I told her, pushing her inside. "You be a good girl. When I get home, you'll have a new friend."

Within a few minutes, Peggy and I were cruising through the pouring rain down Highway 169. "Thank you for coming with me," I said.

I glanced over at my client-turned-friend. Her light red hair looked fuzzy around the edges. Her flawless skin had a porcelain glow. "Love the outfit, by the way. Peach and navy are definitely your colors." I observed her prim slacks and sweater. "I guess you're not planning on riding when we get back?"

"No, I have errands to run." She grinned. "This is a big day for you, though. I can't wait to meet this dog of yours."

"Me, too. It almost seems surreal that he's finally here. His name is Luke, by the way. I don't know where it came from. The name just feels right."

"Luke sounds Biblical," she said. "Do you know what it means?"

"No, now that you mention it. I'll look it up. My aunt Honey had a dictionary of names. She would say, 'A name should reflect someone's strength and personality. A name is a glimpse into the soul.'"

Peggy smiled and nodded. "So, you're going to add sheepherding to horse training. By the way, what did you do before?"

As we merged onto I-44, I turned off the wipers. "Sales manager and gallery designer for a furniture store. Horses have always been my passion, though. I used to sneak off when I was a kid to a horse rental facility a few blocks from our house."

The mention of my aunt Honey and my love of horses produced a motion picture in my mind, and a story came tumbling out.

It was mid-winter in Colorado Springs, Colorado. I was seven years old and standing outside a horse rental facility with my five-year-old brother, Joe.

"Look, Joe, look," I said. "Here they come. I knew it, I knew they would come from the trail."

"I'm cold, sissy. I wanna go home," he whined. "I don't want to see the horses."

I hopped up and down in the snowy slush. "There's a brown one, two white ones, a yellow one, and two black ones. Aren't they beautiful?"

"They ain't etaphants. I'm cold and hungry. I wanna go home."

"It's el-e-phant," I slowly pronounced each syllable. "And Daddy says we're not supposed to say 'ain't.' There *aren't* any elephants."

Joe pulled on my arm. "Not my daddy, my daddy says 'ain't.' I don't care what *your* daddy says. We ain't got a daddy now. I can say what I want."

"I can't wait for Mommy to see them. They're like the ones she draws for me. Only these have saddles and head thingies."

"Mommy draws etaphants for me, and there ain't any here. I wanna go home."

In truth, I was cold too. The walk to the horse stable had been much farther on foot than it had seemed from the school bus. Every day I would sit on the side of the Carver Elementary bus that would face the stable. Maybe, just maybe, I would see someone riding the horses.

While my mother and youngest brother were napping one afternoon, I had convinced my middle brother to go on a great adventure with me. I hadn't been disappointed. People did ride the horses.

Now that I had seen, counted, and knew the colors of every horse in sight, Joe's pleading and my cold feet sent us on our way home.

"There's Mommy," said Joe as we turned the corner onto our street.

"She's going to be so happy," I said. "She can draw lots of horses now, and I can make them all the colors we saw today."

I sprinted toward her. "Mommy, Mommy, guess what's over there." I pointed to the direction we had come from.

Too late, I saw the look on her face. All at once, she grabbed my right arm, jerked me forward, and slapped the left side of my face. I would have hit the ground, but she held my arm in a vice-grip.

"Where have you been?" she screamed. "My check was in the mail. I have to get it cashed so we can eat tonight. I've been out of cigarettes for two days. You're seven years old, old enough to know better, you thoughtless little brat."

"We went to see the horses," I sniffled. "I'm sorry."

"Come on," she snapped. "We have to catch the last bus to the store."

"I told her, Mommy. I told her I was cold and hungry," Joe said as he trotted along behind her.

I held my hot cheek in my hand, choking back sobs as I ran.

Mom trudged with my brother Steve on her hip, dragging Joe by the arm to the corner bus stop.

Once we were seated, I asked, "Can we ride them, Mommy, the horses, all of us together?"

"Thoughtless children like you don't deserve to ride horses. You'd better not ever let me catch you down there again. Now be quiet, or you'll have two red cheeks."

Mother sat in the seat with her legs crossed, one toe twitching in the air, fingers tapping her purse and a tense set to her jaw. She would go without food for us if supplies were low, but she rarely ran out of cigarettes.

I had been thoughtless. Joe and I had eaten the last of the cereal for breakfast. Steve had eaten the last piece of bread. What if I had made us miss the bus to the store? She was right. I felt as if someone squeezed my breath away. I didn't deserve my mother or my brothers.

"I'm so sorry, Mommy," I heard myself say. My heart hurt desperately, but it was at odds with my mind. Images of the horses with riders coming from the trail glided along behind the misery.

When we returned home, Mommy said, "You and Joe put the groceries away. I'll make dinner."

The strained lines faded from her face as cigarette smoke wafted around her head and through our two-room apartment. Her thumb and forefinger plucked a fragment of tobacco from her tongue and flicked it onto the floor. Mom preferred unfiltered Pall Malls.

One corner of our space served as a kitchen. A two-burner stove and oven sat beside a free-standing sink with a red gingham curtain covering the base. My brothers slept on a dingy green pullout sofa bed. Mom and I slept in a full-size bed in a room so small I had to crawl over her to get to the side I slept on.

"Put the labels facing forward," I told Joe. "They have to be tidy."

We stacked cans of Vienna sausages, Spam, chicken noodle soup, and ravioli on one end of the counter.

"Steve," I shouted. "Quit chewing on the Captain Crunch box."
I took the box from my tiny brother and set the treasure beside the packages of powdered milk and jars of Tang. These special items sat on top of the three-foot-tall dorm-style refrigerator that occupied a corner.

On welfare-check day, we feasted on what mom called shit on a shingle, which consisted of packaged chipped beef and white gravy on toast.

The next evening, I was almost asleep when my mother leaned over the bed and touched my shoulder. "I'm going out," she said. "Your brothers are asleep. I'll be home in a few hours."

The only time Mother left us at home alone at night was on Saturday. She would pour herself into her only dress-up dress, a red silk. It clung to her slender shape, showing no signs of the three children she had borne. Her long blond hair left the clean scent of Prell shampoo as it brushed past my face.

"Okay, Mommy." I sat up in the bed. "You look so pretty."

The last sound I heard before going back to sleep were high heels clicking on linoleum. I slept soundly, knowing those heels would be on the floor in the morning and my mom, still in her dress, would be beside me.

But on that cold December morning, her side was horrifyingly empty. No red dress, no shoes, no mother.

"Mommy missed the bus home," I told my brothers. Some little place in my mind told me something was very wrong. But I put on my bossy sister face and made breakfast. We spent the day playing Camelot.

One thing we never argued about was who would play whom. Joe wore a cereal box crown, had a wooden yardstick for a sword, and trotted around the apartment on his great steed of a broom. Steve, being too young to protest, played Guinevere. An old pair of pantyhose fit over his head, allowing the legs to fall down his back for hair. Acting as the wise woman, I wore one of Mom's black dresses, which hung to the floor, and brandished a wooden spoon, casting spells on my brothers.

On Sunday night, I put my brothers to sleep and sat on my bed. I held Felix the Cat to my chest. The tattered black-and-white toy had been my companion for as far back as I could remember. "Mommy will be home by morning," I told my old friend with the plastic blue eyes. "She just has to. I don't know what to do, where to go. She has to be here."

But Monday morning came, and there was still no mother. I wanted to sit on the edge of the bed and sob. Was she okay? Sometimes men came to see her. Was she with one of them? I knew my mother would call if she could, but we didn't have a telephone.

"Okay," I said to myself as I dressed. "She will be here when I get home from school."

After bundling my brothers up in coats, the three of us walked through the twelve inches of snow that still remained against the house until we reached our neighbor Ruth's apartment.

Hers was in the front, ours in the back. She had short red hair, always wore purple lipstick, and smoked her Camel cigarettes through a long plastic filter. No tobacco tongue-picking for her.

"Mommy isn't home," I said to Miss Ruth. "Will you watch my brothers? I have to catch the school bus."

"Sure, sweetie," she said. "But where's your mother?"

"Oh, she must have missed the bus home cuz of the snow." I looked out the window, averting my eyes.

Ruth's mouth got very round. "Look at you, child. Did you get that wrinkled-up thing out of the dirty clothes hamper? You look like a ragamuffin."

I had pulled the pink-and-white seersucker dress from a pile on the floor. My face flushed hot and my ears burned while I ran my hands over the offending wrinkles.

"Come here," Ruth chided. "Take that off." She took a robe from a hook on the back of her bedroom door and handed it to me. Then she gave both of my brothers a cookie. They sat quietly on her living room floor, munching their treats.

Ruth's apartment was slightly larger than ours, and an ironing board sat perpetually between her kitchen area and living room. She plugged in her iron and shook the water-filled RC Cola bottle over my garment.

"Don't you know how to use an iron?" Ruth asked.

"I do, but Mommy left it on the counter of our old house. I think the note she wrote to Daddy said something about where Daddy could put the iron, and that he could press his own uniforms. She probably said under the sink, The sun doesn't shine in there."

Ruth didn't laugh. She cackled, a high-pitched sound that made me think someone had tickled a chicken. Startled, my brothers looked up from the floor. I shrugged and gave them a look that said, "I think she might be a little touched."

My neighbor was still smiling when the wrinkle-free dress slipped over my head. Then, her smile vanished. Momentarily confused, I followed her gaze downward.

The dirty white Keds I wore were too small, and my big toe had worn a hole in my left shoe. My feet were cold and soaked from the walk to the front of the house. Thinking of the shoes and the wrinkled dress, I realized with horror that I hadn't brushed my long blond hair. Humiliation wasn't a strong enough word to describe what I felt. I wished with all my heart I could simply fall through the floor.

"You can't wear those," said Ruth. "Let me see what I can find." She muttered something to herself about women's attraction to military men as she moved boxes around in a closet.

A vision of my father hammered through my mind.

Sergeant First Class Robert L. Wedding insisted on the tidiness of a military barracks. "Daddy will be home in two hours," Mother would say. "Get busy, you little munchkins."

The three of us would rush around, cleaning up. We could have passed for Robert Young's family on the *Father Knows Best* sitcom with our clean clothes, orderly house, and impeccable manners. Except ours would have been *Family Becoming a Military Officer.*

"Oh, Miss Ruth," I cried. "I'm unbecoming… Look at me." I gazed around Ruth's tiny, clean apartment. I didn't want her to see our house. Merlin, King Arthur, and Guinevere had left our castle in chaos.

"My father could never love me like this." Nausea threatened, and I clasped my hand over my mouth. It felt as if a family of writhing worms were camped out in my stomach.

"Now, don't believe that for a second, child," Ruth said. "That man is far across the ocean, and nothing he says can hurt you or your mom."

But I knew what it was to be a child of an important man, and I still craved his approval. "Your mommy is doing the best she can." Ruth set a pair of black-and-white saddle shoes on the floor. "Here, put these on. They will be a little big." She handed me two pairs of clean white socks.

"Miss Ruth, these are beautiful." The socks felt like heaven as I slipped my red toes inside. After I tied the shoes, I clicked my heels, feeling like Dorothy in *The Wizard of Oz*.

Ruth brushed my hair. "There." She smiled. "You're the most becoming young lady I know... a princess, even. Now, get your brothers. I'll take you to school."

Kids were exiting the school bus when we drove up.

"I knew you had to have missed that bus," said Ruth. "I'll keep your brothers for the day, but I'll have to go to work later. The roads are clear, so your mother should be home anytime."

"Thank you, oh, thank you, Miss Ruth. I'll hurry when school is out." I alternated looking down at my feet with running my fingers through my tangle-free long hair. I did feel becoming.

I squared my shoulders and walked into the classroom, wishing for the first time that someone would notice me. I puffed out my chest and smiled. Mommy would be home when I got there, and life was wonderful.

The moment I sat down on the window side of the afternoon school bus, my becoming-princess euphoria ebbed away. I sank into the seat like pudding. What would we do if Mommy wasn't there?

As I walked down the block from the bus, my heart leapt. I laughed and took off at a sprint. A powder-blue 1957 Chevrolet was parked in the street in front of our house.

"My-Honey, My-Honey," I shouted as I ran through the door.

Mother's oldest sister sat my brother Steve down and wrapped me in a hug. My head lay on her ample bosom, and I instantly melted into a sense of security. As her strong arms encircled my body, I knew everything would be okay.

Her name, Evelyn, had been difficult for me to pronounce when I was small, so I had dubbed her My-Honey.

"Let me look at you," My-Honey said, holding my shoulders. "You've grown up." Then, she wrapped her arms around me again. "Oh, sweetheart, I missed you so."

"Where's Mommy?" I asked, looking around. Certainly, my aunt had driven from California to see her.

"We will talk about that," My-Honey replied. "You need to gather your clothes and belongings. The three of you are coming to live with me."

"We can't leave without Mommy," I said. My voice climbed octaves by the second. "What's happened to her?"

My-Honey placed my small hands in hers. "Eva is okay. She's been institutionalized."

I felt the scar on my forehead lift and wrinkle in question.

"A type of hospital," said My-Honey. "Your Mommy can't have visitors for a while. She tried to take her own life. She's very sick now, but she will be stable soon, and we will move her to a facility in California. Then you can see her."

"Did I do something?" I choked. "Doesn't she want us? I won't sneak off to the horses anymore."

It hadn't taken long for me to know what times the rental horses left and returned to the stable each day. If I planned very carefully, I could leave my brothers just long enough to see the sacred animals with their riders. Had my mother known I had been sneaking down there? Was she very angry with me?

"Goodness, no, your mother loves all of you very much. She simply couldn't cope with some of the things in her life. Things that have nothing to do with the three of you."

"Sissy took me to the horses, and I got cold," said Joe, then began to cry. "I want to see my mommy."

My-Honey reached down, picked up Joe, and hugged him. "You

will see your mommy when she's all better. In the meantime, take Steve into the bathroom and wash his face and hands, please."

The next morning the four us left for California. Mother came to live with us nine months later.

My father never came back into our lives. I did write, but my letters were returned with a note that said, "Your penmanship is unacceptable. Do not write again until it has improved."

Peggy and I rode in silence for several long minutes. I felt raw and embarrassed. Sharing one of my dysfunctional family stories was the last thing I had expected to fill the driving time.

Peggy finally said, "You know what strikes me about your story is the contradictions in your upbringing—going from a strict military structure to being poor and living in what could only be described as poverty. It says a lot, that you have accomplished what you have." Then she laughed. "The first time I entered your barn. I went home and told my husband it was as clean and organized as a military barracks."

Chuckling, I added, "I still won't wear Keds tennis shoes. And don't even talk about how picky I am about clothes."

"So, where's the rest of your family, mother, brothers?" Peggy tucked an errant piece of hair behind her ear. "The only one you speak about is Honey."

"Mom passed during open-heart surgery several years ago. She meant well when we were kids, she just had some hurdles in her life she couldn't jump. My-Honey was my rock, my security, but she passed last year. My brother Joe died of a drug overdose. Steve lives in Hawaii and is doing well."

"Seems pretty impossible to me," Peggy's emerald eyes held a silent statement of support, "that you have a successful marriage, a great daughter, your own business. How" she took in an audible breath, "did you get here, in Oklahoma, doing all this?"

"Well, let me see… My fifth stepdad, Tom Payne, took a job in

Oklahoma and moved us all here. He was a really good man. He passed last year, too. For most of my high school years, Mom was in some kind of rehab. Tom tried to care for my brothers and me but he worked two jobs to support us. I guess I'm a Cal-Okie—as an adult, I moved back and forth several times."

"You," Peggy said, "are amazing."

"Thanks." I glanced at her. "My childhood wasn't a pretty one, or a happy one, or a comfortable one. It simply was. It didn't feel good to live in my story, so I lived in my head."

An awareness overcame me. "Peggy," I gasped. "Many of the things that I would spend hours imagining have come into my life. I had a black-and-white Felix the Cat as a kid, and I would run my hands through its fake fur. To me, the toy represented the Border Collie puppies I never got to play with. It felt like heaven."

Smiling at another memory, I went on, "I could ride a horse in my mind for hours, feeling all the different gates: walking, trotting, galloping. Oh man, one of my most treasured possessions was a pair of old cotton gloves. One of My-Honey's friends let me pet their horses. The smell of them brought horses to life in my mind."

"Hum," Peggy said. "What's that Albert Einstein quote? Nothing is ever created that isn't first imagined? Maybe you're right. Oh, there's Eighty-First Street. In just a few minutes, we'll meet your new dog. I bet he's as beautiful as you imagined."

Chapter Seven

We drove through gullies of water as we entered Stan Abernathy's veterinary clinic parking lot. Rain droplets splashed onto a black Chevy pickup parked under a giant oak tree.

"Looks like they're here," Peggy said.

Dr. Stan stood at the door of the clinic, talking to a dark-haired man who was a full head shorter and quite a bit stockier than he.

As I parked beside the black truck, the sun broke through the clouds. "That must be Charlie," I said. A wet stainless steel crate shone in the broken light and caught my eye. Peering through the tiny window was an eye, followed by an ear, then a nose. "That's a dog in there." That dog must have ridden in the back of the truck all the way from Arkansas, through the pounding rain, lighting, and thunder, all by himself. Disbelief blended with comprehension. "That's my dog!" My voice pitched high with sudden anger.

My first instinct was to storm up to the man I took to be Charlie and scream, "What kind of an ogre could treat my dog like that?" But I took a few deep breaths and channeled my emotions back to safe ground.

"Working dogs are handled differently than pets sometimes," Peggy said. "I wouldn't like it either, but that's the way they are."

Dr. Stan smiled, waved, and walked back into his clinic.

The dark-haired man walked over to Peggy and me as we came around the back of my truck.

"Hi, I'm Charlie," he said with a big, toothy smile.

That was the voice from the phone—that resonate baritone I loved to listen to. I stood mute as the voice and the ogre image warred in my mind.

Peggy extended her hand. "Glad to meet you. I'm Naomi's friend."

Charlie turned to me. "You must be Naomi?"

Still smiling, his eyes narrowed when I didn't respond with a smile. He lowered the tailgate. "Um, the pup's back here," he said and jumped into the back of the truck. "Sorry I didn't have time to clean him up."

Peggy and I lowered our heads to peer inside the door as Charlie opened it. All we could see was a strip of white, a shiny black nose, and two huge eyes—striking eyes, dark brown, circled with large whites. Then, the nose and eyes turned toward the back of the crate as if to say, "If I can't see you, maybe you'll go away."

"Doesn't look like he's coming out on his own." Charlie reached in, grabbed the dog's paws, and pulled him out onto the truck bed with a wet plop.

The smell of wet dog and stagnate pond water made me feel sick.

As Peggy gasped and stepped back, I scrambled onto the truck bed and gathered the shaking, stinking mass of fur in my arms. When I found it, my voice came out in a whisper. "Luke, my Luke... how could you treat him this way?"

"Ah, I don't think he hurt himself in there," answered Charlie, sounding confused. "You're getting your clothes filthy and smelly. When I let him out to run, he always heads to the pond. Dives right in up to his eyeballs and swims along like an alligator or something. Never seen one do that but him."

Peggy climbed up onto the truck bed. "It's okay, sweet boy. My, aren't you handsome under all that smell and wet."

"Look, like I said, you don't have to take him." Charlie glanced at the back of my truck. "Where's your crate?"

All sorts of snarky retorts passed through my mind. I wanted to yell about callous, inconsiderate ogres who made a young dog take his first ride in the back of a truck during a horrible storm. But before I could form a cohesive thought, a sudden bark and the sound of paws thumping against the back window of the truck startled me out of my thoughts.

"Casper, that'll do. Quiet," Charlie said as he opened the back door. A snow-white Jack Russell Terrier jumped out and sat silently at his side.

"Over there… Do your business." The dog ran over to the appointed direction, relieved himself, and came back. "Good boy. Load up."

Casper jumped onto the seat and watched us through the back window.

The pause had given me time to harness my emotions and think about my words. I wouldn't be able to take them back: words to Stan's friend, words to Charlie whom I had come to like and respect during our phone conversations, words to the man that Casper obviously loved and obeyed. "I didn't think I would need a crate," I said carefully. "I don't own one."

As Charlie considered my answer, comprehension shone through his eyes and he gave a slight smile.

"Naomi, my understanding is that you want a working dog, a competition dog. Granted, this one is shyer than most and might not work out. But cattle and sheep dogs work in all weather conditions, in all sorts of terrain. You can't treat them like a pampered pet and expect them to get the job done when circumstances get tough. I've rarely seen a herding trial cancelled because of weather."

I nodded. He made sense. I had made a commitment to buy this dog months ago. "His name is Luke," I said. All at once, a stab of fear coursed through me as I thought, *Buy this dog.* I had forgotten all about the "buying" part.

Research had shown me that a trained dog could cost anywhere from $1000 to $3500, and a well-bred, unstarted dog would be anywhere from $500 to $1500. Charlie's voice had been full of pride for his dog's imported pedigree and their success on the trial field and on his working ranch. How could I have not thought about such an important factor? What if I didn't have enough to buy Luke?

My arms wrapped tighter around the shaking, stinking, furry being in my lap. Trying to keep my voice light, I said, "I feel silly. I never asked you how much you want for him."

"Well, we haven't talked about that, have we?" Charlie gazed off as if he were mentally calculating the national debt.

This dog was mine. I knew it. He had to be. My mind raced in desperation. I could sell something if I had to. I could offer some service. I could… I held my breath.

Finally, after what felt like an eternity, he said, "How about fifty dollars? Take him now and send me a check if you decide to keep him."

My jaw almost dropped, but I hid the wave of relief that washed over me. What if he realized what an absurd deal it was and take it back? *Fifty dollars?* Was I dreaming?

Peggy quickly said, "He can sit in my lap if you don't have something to cover your seats."

A few minutes later, we were driving home with my new dog, his registration papers, and the name of a woman who gave herding lessons and also trained dogs.

After a few minutes of thoughtful silence, Peggy said, "That was interesting. Not what you expected, I'm sure." She looked at Luke in her lap. "He's still shaking, but he seems sweet. Hard to imagine an animal so well-bred in this condition."

I sighed and said, "I don't know what to think. But I do know there was no way I would let him go back with Charlie."

"Well," Peggy said. "Maybe he will be a playmate for Bobbie Jo. I have to say, he does look more like a barn dog than your Lhasa Apso." She gave a slight chuckle, then said in a serious tone, "I'm afraid you're going to be disappointed." She stroked Luke's back. "It's hard to imagine this pitiful thing ever having the confidence a herding dog needs."

"Oh, please don't put any more doubts in my mind. The ones already there don't need company. My fragile hope for this dog couldn't survive it." I shook my head and gave her a weak smile.

We sat in silence for the rest of the drive home. Just before we turned in to my place, Luke stopped shaking and mustered up enough courage to glance up at Peggy. Then he tilted his head to me. He didn't flinch when I stroked between his ears. Encouraged, I did it again.

Chapter Eight

T he shavings delivery truck stood parked in front of the barn
when we arrived home. I pulled in next to the property line fence,
squinting through the light rain. I fumbled with my hood and jacket
zipper as I walked around to the back of the truck.

"Luke probably needs to pee," Peggy said, bending to set him on
the ground.

"No!" I shouted... but it was too late.

In a flash, he was running across the pasture like a crazed jackrabbit,
through the cable fence and into my neighbor's field. Instantly, fear
gripped me. "There are hundreds of acres of farmland and woods
around us," I gasped. "If he makes it that far, I'll never see him again."

But Peggy was already gone, running through the fence to keep
him in sight.

Seeing her jolted me into action. I took off after them. My pursuit
didn't last long. As I vaulted through the two cables, my spur got caught
on the top one. I face-planted in wet grass, leaves, and mud.

"Keep going," I yelled. "I'm okay." I spit dirt from my mouth as I
stumbled back to my feet.

Every so often, we caught a glimpse of a white-tipped tail as he
ran... and ran... and ran.

My panicked heartbeat thumped at a rate that probably matched his as he sped past the cows, past the Miller family farm, past their paddocks, and into their barn.

"Did you see that?" Peggy yelled. "We can catch him in there. I hope there isn't a back way out."

By the time we entered the barn, we were heaving big gulps of air, our soaked clothing dripping puddles on the floor. I bent and put my hands on my knees. A quick scan told me there was no other way out. Tools and cleaning implements hung on the wall by the front door. Several hundred bales of hay were stacked to the rafters at the back of the barn. "He's got to be in here," I panted.

Horses occupied four stalls on the left. They nickered and moved around as we entered. "It's not feeding time yet, guys," I said. "Hey, can any of you tell us where the black-and-white dog is?"

Peggy chuckled. "I wish they could."

We had been searching unsuccessfully for quite a while when I noticed a flashlight on a shelf. My nose was suddenly drawn to a scent by the hay—wet dog and stagnate pond water.

I shone the flashlight toward the aroma and saw the light reflected by two huge eyes and a white-striped face.

"There you are," I said, kneeling on the ground. "Ah, sweetie, how did you get way back there?" The dog was wedged into a small opening in the haystack, with seven rows of hay above him.

"Oh, man," Peggy muttered. "How are we going to get him out of there? Even if we could reach him, he might bite out of fear."

As I scrubbed my forehead with my fingertips, I looked around, willing some brilliant idea to appear.

"Food probably won't work," I said.

Peggy smirked. "Yeah, right."

"Okay, I'm going to move the entire front row of bales so I can lift him out. Why don't you sit by the opening in case he bolts?"

"I guess there's no other way." Peggy sat down on the floor and bent to say, "Hey, pretty boy, we're going to get you out of there. Get you home and some food." Her sing-song voice sounded soft and soothing.

Tightly wound with strands of wire, the seventy-pound bales

bounced when they hit the concrete floor. Concerned that one might hit Peggy, I rolled them off to the side. The lower ones weren't so easy. I had to lift and place them beside her. Blisters soon formed on my fingers. Every few minutes, I stopped to shake my hands. Soon, my arms felt as if they were on fire.

"You look like the Incredible Hulk," Peggy said, grinning.

I pulled myself up to my full five foot five inches, one hundred ten pounds, and flexed my muscles. "Gee, I'm flattered. But green isn't my color."

My hair and clothes were sweat soaked by the time I finally reached down and wrapped my arms around Luke. "Hi, there. I'm going to set you in Peggy's lap, okay?" I told him.

Once she had secured the still-shaking animal, I collapsed beside her. "Now what?"

"It's a mile back to the house," Peggy said. "He's too big to carry. We could use a lead rope around his neck, but then we would have to drag the petrified thing. And listen…" She pointed up. The rain hitting the metal roof sounded like BBs.

"We can't call anyone to come get us," I said. "Our phones and purses are in the truck. I'll go through the pasture and bring it back."

Peggy shivered.

"Your jacket is in the truck too." I picked up the jacket I had taken off and wrapped it around her shoulders. "Here, I'm still hot."

"You can't go out in the rain without protection," she protested, trying to hand the jacket back.

"I'll be fine. Look." I pointed to a neatly stacked pile of empty blue-and-white feed sacks. "Those empty fifty-pound sacks for horse pellets are lined with plastic." I grabbed a pair of shears from the wall hook and cut one of the sacks up the front almost to the top, then placed it over my head. The sides hung down to my waist. "See, instant raincoat," I said, modeling. "I'll go get the truck."

That's when I remembered the No Trespassing signs posted all along Mr. Miller's fence. The Miller house stood a mile down a gravel road. They liked their privacy.

"I'd better stop and tell Mr. Miller what happened. We don't want him to think he's been vandalized."

"Oh, yes." A lopsided grin curled up Peggy's lips. "He's been vandalized by a soggy redheaded woman and an equally soggy dog."

That made us both giggle, which quickly exploded into bubbling laughter. Punch-drunk tears left streaks on our dirt-smudged faces.

Luke's head jerked up, his eyes wide with panic. He tried to squirm out of Peggy's lap.

"I'm sorry. I'm sure you've never seen a laughing feed sack," I chuckled, taking off the offending makeshift raincoat. "Poor thing must think he's gone to a crazy farm."

Slowly, I bent down and ran my hand over his back. Then I lifted his face with the other hand and gazed into those human-like eyes. I felt a sudden pulse of love so palpable it took my breath away. My entire body rang with a fierce, joyous serenity of purpose. The doors of my heart opened, and I knew my decision hadn't been wrong. He was my Luke, and he was here to stay.

As I walked toward the door, I glanced back at the lady seated cross-legged on the barn floor with a dog in her lap. "I'm so sorry your clothes got ruined. Thanks for being such a good friend."

Peggy flashed me a generous smile that lit up her whole face, then continued to sing a soft lullaby while stroking Luke's fur.

The light rain sounded like tiny woodpeckers on the heavy paper sack that covered my head and shoulders as I sprinted home.

A beat-up blue Honda Civic sat next to my truck. Sharon, my helper, must have arrived while I was searching for my dog.

"Where have you been?" she shouted in a deep, gravelly voice while stomping down the barn aisle like an enraged bantam hen. She waved a lime-green pooper-scooper at me. "I've been scared to death. Peggy's car is here, but no Peggy. Your truck's parked in the wrong place. Two purses and phones in the seat... No sign of you."

I felt my eyes grow round as her tirade went on.

"I didn't know if you'd been hurt and left in an ambulance, or if someone had taken you! Were you abducted by aliens?"

The short, thin, well-muscled woman ranting before me not only cleaned my barn six days a week but also did the same at the Claremore Racetrack. Her fierce look told me to hide the mirth that bubbled in my throat.

Suddenly, the shouting ceased, and Sharon tilted her head as if seeing me for the first time. She cackled. "Why do you have a feed sack on your head?"

"Don't laugh at my new raincoat." I held myself erect with my hands on my hips. I gave her the brief version of how we lost and found my new dog.

Sharon leaned the pooper-scooper against a wall. "Let's go retrieve Peggy and the dog. I'll help you restack the hay."

Mr. Miller was in the barn when Sharon and I returned. Soon, the hay was restacked, and I was finally on my way home with the animal that would change my life forever.

"Put him in that first stall on the left," Sharon said as I carried Luke into the barn. "He can't escape from in there."

With Luke secured in the stall, Peggy and Sharon cared for the horses and left.

Luke nosed around and settled in the clean shavings with his head facing the corner.

I slid the door open, crept in, closed it again, and sat down with my back against the opposite wall. My body felt limp and tired as a wrung-out dishrag.

"Well, here we are. We're quite a pair."

"That's an understatement," came a voice from above my head. "I thought you wanted a herding dog. You two look more like a mud-wrestling duo." Mac came in and joined me on the floor. He sniffed and said, "My lord, were you wrestling in a fishpond?"

"No, he came smelling like this." I had been with Luke so long I had become olfactory-blind. "We've had a day you wouldn't believe."

It took twenty minutes to recount my day, including my anger at Charlie, Peggy's witticisms about the Incredible Hulk, and the coyote in the pasture. "I'm exhausted," I finished.

"Yes, you both need a shower. I'll help you with him in the wash stall. But I want to tell you something first." Mac picked a piece of hay out of my hair. His fingers brushed my face with a light touch as he gave me a smile as warm as a summer sunset. "You're disappointed, and who wouldn't be? But if anyone can bring out what's hidden under all that timid grunge, it's you. I've seen you take customers' horses and bring out the best in them time after time—horses I wouldn't have given two cents for. You not only make them something, you teach their owners how to do the same. Do what you always do. Take it one step at a time."

I smiled. "Thank you. You're right. You have to be right. My sheep dog is in there somewhere just waiting to be washed, trained, and loved."

Luke hadn't moved but had watched us warily while we spoke. When all was quiet except for horse sounds—drinking water, munching hay, the occasional squeal at a neighbor—the three of us relaxed into peaceful silence. No longer trembling, Luke rested his chin on his paws.

Here we go, I thought. *One step at a time.*

"Will you carry him to the wash stall?" I asked. "We'll use the horse shampoo and conditioner. There's some lavender oil on the shelf that we can rub on his ears. It might help him relax."

Fifteen minutes later, Mac was in the kitchen, toweling Luke dry.

Hot water and essential oil soap flowed over my skin, taking the stench of pond water, grass, and dirt with it. Lemon, eucalyptus, rosemary, and aloe soothed my tired muscles and frayed nerves. "He drank some water, but he hasn't eaten as far as I know," I said as I stood in the doorway, toweling my hair.

"He ate a little while you showered," Mac replied. "Mostly, he just goes to any hidey-hole he can find. I've pulled him out of two."

"We can close the bedroom door," I said. "Then he can't escape."

Closing the door did prevent him from escaping, but didn't stop him from finding a new hidey-hole: the nook between the wall and armoire. With Bobbie Jo struggling to free herself from Mac's arms, Mac and I stared at Luke from the bed.

"At least he's consistent," Mac said. "He has hidey-hole radar." He grimaced, holding wriggling Bobbie. "She really wants down. I can hardly hold on to her."

"Hey, handsome." I moved to the floor and extended the back of my hand toward Luke. "What a pretty boy you are." His cold nose brushed my fingers. "Want to meet Bobbie Jo? She's your new sister. You'll really like her."

"I don't think that's wise," said Mac. "How do you know you can trust him not to hurt her?"

"This dog has had the most traumatic day of his life, and not one time has he growled or threatened to bite. Let her down. I can grab her if there's trouble."

Holding our breath, poised to move, we watched both dogs crouch nose to nose, staring each other down. Then, in one mouth-dropping moment, Bobbie Jo jumped straight up and landed on Luke's head.

Lightning-quick, Mac dove for them.

But Luke was faster. He vaulted from the corner, dislodging Bobbie Jo, and spun around to land in play-pose. Both dogs crouched on their front paws, their tails wagging like windmills. Once all the important body parts had been sniffed, toenails were clicking in a rapid staccato on the green cement floor as the dogs chased each other around the room.

"Look how careful he is with her. She's loving having someone to play with even if he is so much bigger." Relief washed over me as I saw some semblance of a normal dog.

After Bobbie Jo lay cuddled up between us, I said, "Charlie must have socialized him with other dogs. It seems people are the problem. At least we know there's someone he's comfortable with."

When Luke had once again curled up in the corner, I turned off the lights. Mac and I lay side by side, holding hands and gazing silently up at the moonlit ceiling.

My mind wouldn't shut down. It kept reliving the events from the day. I went back to the jingle-clank-whirr of the tractor with the soiled shavings spraying into the air and landing on the earth. I could see new sprouts of bluestem grass glistening with raindrops. I thought about the confusion, the self-doubt, and the uncertainty. An idea crystalized, and I chuckled softly.

"What's that about?" Mac asked.

"I thought you were asleep," I whispered. "My brain doesn't seem to know how tired my body is. But I had a thought."

"Well?"

"Well, my whole life has been like manure."

"You don't smell all the time, just some of the time."

I heard the mirth hidden in his words, so I did what I often did. I smiled, shook my head, and pretended he didn't say them. "Here's the thing. We cut the hay. The horses eat it. We pick it out of the stalls, only to put it back on the earth. Then, the whole process starts all over again." I sighed. "It's just like me. I work on my emotional stuff, the self-doubt, and the fear of going forward. Life gets better, and I think all that's behind me. I'm confident in what I do, and think I have the world figured out, and… boom, I start something new and it all sprouts back up." I looked at him. "See?"

"Come here." Mac moved Bobbie Jo to his other side and opened his arm in invitation.

I snuggled in under it and lay my head in the indention between his shoulder and chest, which always felt like it had been designed for me only. As I relaxed into him, I sighed.

"Aw, honey," Mac said. "I always knew I'd be married to someone special." His tone grew serious. "I can just see you in a Hindu robe with spurs extending from the hem, emitting a luminous glow as manure flies out behind you."

His chest vibrated with his chuckle. I punched it and went to sleep.

Chapter Nine

Three weeks later, I opened the back door of my truck and shouted, "Luke, here." He came bounding up from the backyard, Bobbie Jo close behind. "Load up. It's time to go to Mandy's for our first sheep lesson."

My dog leapt from the ground to the backseat, which was now fitted with washable covers.

"What a good guy you are." I scooped up Bobbie Jo in one hand and roughed Luke's neck with the other. His entire body wagged at the praise. My heart did a little twitter at our accomplishment.

When I could see that Luke and I were bonding and that, in fact, he was smart and learned quickly, I called the woman that Charlie had had recommended for herding training.

"So, you have one of Charlie Cameron's dogs," Mandy Weis had said. "They're well-bred for sure. From what I've see of them, they're plenty biddable."

"Biddable?"

"It's a term used by herding trainers," she had replied. "A biddable dog is obedient and is willing to follow instructions. A herding dog needs to be confident and aggressive, but they also must be biddable or trainable. If not, you have no control. My place is close to the Arkansas border, just outside of Springdale. Nine months old is a good time to start them. I have some mature ewes that make it easy for a young dog. If you want to bring him, I'll see what you have."

After questioning Mandy at length about her training practices, I had agreed to bring Luke and introduce him to her sheep. "What should he know before we come?"

"Just have a lay down, a recall, and a few other things. The rest we teach with the sheep. Let me give you a list of do's and don'ts."

Mandy had been emphatic when she said, "Most working dogs don't sleep in human houses. Erect a sturdy kennel in a place where he will not be able to see the sheep when you get them. It can confuse him if he sees livestock and isn't allowed to approach them."

Mac had spent the following Saturday erecting the best portable kennel Owasso, Oklahoma, had to offer, along with a wall-to-wall rubber floor and a climate-controlled, insulated igloo doghouse. He had even placed a small fence and plants around it so it blended with the landscaping of our backyard. "Well, here's your Taj Mahal kennel. I hope he likes it."

That evening, Luke spent about ten minutes in his stunning new dwelling. He went into the doghouse, turned around, lay down, and rested his chin on his paws. The resignation in his eyes was unmistakable. His expression clearly said, "You're abandoning me here."

"Well, he seems to be okay," Mac said. "I'm sure it's better than what he had before... Uh-oh. Your eyes are glossed over. He's not staying out here, is he?"

I shook my head. "I'm sorry. You built it, and it's so beautiful. But... but... I can't do it. I can't leave him."

Mac sucked in a breath and stood in tense silence for what seemed a very long time. Anger, tested patience, and finally gentle amusement crossed his face. "Okay, gather up your dog."

"Come here, sweetie." I wrapped Luke in my arms. "You will never spend another night alone in a kennel. Let's go in the house." Lifting his head, I said, "I won't tell Mandy if you don't."

Luke's progress was encouraging. He and Bobbie Jo played often.

Mac grew to love him too. The frightened, timid dog had become a member of our family. My doubts about him lessened every day.

However, he continued to find nooks and crevices to hide in. To stop Luke's hidey-hole habit, I attached a thirteen-foot line to his collar. Whenever he found a hole, a light tug, a treat, and a pet would bring him out. After a few days, he followed me everywhere, but his only real freedom to run was in the closed-up barn.

Finally, I unhooked the line and let him go.

Every day we worked on Mandy's list until we had them all ticked off. Luke came when called, lay down when asked, and walked beside me on a leash. He was comfortable on a tether, but nothing eased his fear of someone approaching. He never growled or attempted to nip or bite, only barked a ferocious bark that would startle anyone and send them in the opposite direction.

Whenever Sharon came into view, Luke went ballistic. After several weeks of this, Sharon's face tightened in irritation. "He needs to quit barking at me every time I come around a corner. Makes me jump out of my skin."

"He's not afraid of you or Mac; he barks at everyone but me. I hope it's a temporary quirk. Will you let Bobbie Jo out before you go?"

The little dog squirmed in my arms as I closed the truck door and walked toward the house with her. I called to Sharon, "She knows Luke is going and not her. She isn't happy."

Sharon's face softened. "Sure, she likes to bring the horses in with me. I'll leave by three. I have to pick up both my kids from school."

"Thanks. I'll see you in the morning."

Springdale, Arkansas, was ninety minutes from Owasso. It made for a beautiful drive through southern Oklahoma in October, underneath trees ablaze in golds, yellows, and reds.

The path to Mandy's was full of gravel roads and missing road signs, meaning I nearly passed the red barn I was supposed to be aiming for. As I hit the brakes and backed up, an enormous cloud of dust engulfed a girl's pink bike that leaned against a tree.

I grimaced as I glanced in the rearview mirror. "Sorry."

High winds from the night before had given the maple trees one of nature's trim jobs. The driveway had not only a brilliant canopy but also a colorful carpet of leaves. I felt as if I were entering an artist's rendering of a perfect fall day in the country. The pallet of fall color blended perfectly against a clear blue sky. The white rail fencing was the finishing touch.

A woman stood at the end of the drive and motioned toward a spot for me to park. Once out of the truck, I paused to take in a myriad of contrasts. The woman had a long, wavy blond ponytail and slightly canted brown eyes. We shook hands, and I noticed her perfectly manicured red fingernails. She wore a faded plaid flannel shirt and dirty jeans.

I looked around. A brick ranch home sat in a massive green lawn. Behind the house, a long building had small doorways leading into individual kennel enclosures where seven dogs rested.

Yapping loudly, a long-haired dachshund stopped at the woman's feet.

"Hi, I'm Mandy," the woman said. "This is Frizzle, resident guide, protector, and foo-foo dog."

Frizzle was a blue-gray color with black spots. She looked up at me with one blue eye and one brown one. When she moved, her coat swept the ground like a feather duster.

"It's beautiful here," I said. I leaned down to see Frizzle better, and asked, "What's a foo-foo dog."

Mandy's eyes grew wide, as if the question took her by surprise. "A nonworking dog." She reached down and stroked the spotted long-haired creature at her feet. "You have important jobs, huh, Frizzle? You sit beside me when I watch television, sleep in my bed, snore... and you're the best cuddler ever." Mandy looked back at me. "If you want a working or competition dog to perform at their best, they are *not* treated like foo-foo dogs."

"Oh, I see." I quickly moved to my truck. *Well, Luke doesn't sleep in my bed, if that's any concession.* As if on cue, he whined from the backseat.

"This is Luke," I told Mandy. "It might seem small, but to us, it's huge that he didn't run to the other side of the truck when I opened the door."

Mandy frowned, as if holding a comment back.

I wondered if riding in the backseat of trucks would also fall in the foo-foo dog category. It would have in Charlie's opinion.

Once the leash clicked onto Luke's collar, he jumped down, stood at my side, and promptly peed on my leg.

The warm liquid hit my calf just below my capris and ran into my tennis shoe. Luke jumped to the end of his leash at my startled hop. He spun in an effort to get under my truck, but I held on firmly with the long leash wrapped around one of my legs.

Mandy shook her head and said with mirth in her tone, "Well, if you're finished playing Laurel and Hardy, I'll get you a towel to wipe that off."

Heat rose up my chest to my cheeks. I untangled myself from my dog and reached for the rag on my floorboard. "I have one right here. I can't believe he did that."

"Ah, he's insecure and marked you as his. You attached a leash to him, and he decided to connect to you with an invisible one. Come on, let's walk down to the sheep pen and see what you have in Luke here."

Bending down, I took Luke's face in my hands. "Hey, buddy, let's go work some sheep."

Frizzle led the way at a trot, fluffy tail held high, ears bouncing, and nose straight ahead. Clearly, she had done this before.

The acrid scent of sheep manure caught a ride on the breeze as it blew past our faces. Luke's ears perked up, and he looked toward a large, round wire pen that held three smooth-coated brown animals.

"I thought sheep were white and wooly," I said. "Those are flat coated and brown. There is even a brown-and-white one. Looks like a tiny paint horse."

"They are St. Croix," Mandy replied as she approached the gate. "They have good temperaments, and they have hair, so they shed. No shearing required."

"Don't you want the wool?"

Mandy walked into the pen and removed a rubber feed tub. "People don't wear wool clothing anymore. Shearing is hot, messy business, and there's no money in it unless you have huge herds. I keep only about thirty at a time, so I use St. Croix. After I get out, you and your dog walk in. Just let him do what comes natural."

Luke and I went into the enclosure and stood against the fence. I felt awkward, and my heart moved to my throat. Exercising an untethered horse in the same type of round pen was something I did often. I knew where to place my body to move the horse forward, toward me, or away from me. I could read their emotions and body language. Here I was completely out of my element.

Three sheep… Should we try to move just one? What if Luke got close and they charged at him? What if they charged me? Could I wave my arms and keep them away from him? They were so small. What's the worst thing that could happen? Knock me down, I suppose. Dog urine already soaked my shoe; what would be a little sheep poop on my butt?

"You can take the leash off your dog anytime now."

Mandy's voice startled me. "I feel silly. I have no idea what to do." I looked at her and back at the sheep to see if they moved at the sound of her voice.

The doe-faced creatures stood completely still on the other side of the pen, waiting for us to do something.

"Your dog should have the instinct. We are here to see if he does. Let him go."

The word *instinct* jolted me. Innate drive, and the beauty of it, was why I loved the sport of herding. "I just realized something," I exclaimed with a laugh. "I've waited almost half my life for a herding dog. And here we are: Luke, me, and sheep."

Mandy crossed her arms. "We're probably never going to know if he has the instinct if you keep talking us into old age."

"Oops. I do that when I'm nervous." My hands shook as I unsnapped the leash.

Luke sat completely still.

Mandy stood with her arms folded on the top fence rail. "You walk toward the sheep. The motion will get them moving. That should spark his interest."

I did as Mandy instructed. However, Luke took every step with me. "Okay, mister, it's your time," I told him. "This is what you were bred for." I waved my arms in the air and clapped my hands, and the sheep trotted along the fence line. Instantly, Luke moved away from me and behind them. My face erupted into a huge smile. "There he goes."

Then, his nose went to the ground to smell poop. The sheep stopped.

"That can happen with a young dog," Mandy encouraged me. "Keep them moving."

"Okay."

From up the leaf-coated gravel drive came a small girl's voice. "Mom, my bike's covered with dust again. My butt's dirty." The girl was around eight years old, tiny in stature, with pixie-like hair and the same eyes as her mother. She stopped the bike by the fence.

"It's bottom, dear. You know to keep a rag in your basket. Now go to the house. I won't be long." The girl rode off down the drive.

Mandy turned her attention back to me. "Where did your dog go?"

During the exchange, I hadn't noticed Luke was gone.

My dog had huddled in an indention in the fence.

"Get those ewes moving again," Mandy ordered. "It should draw him out."

"The dust culprit was me," I said. "I stopped my truck and backed up. Tell her I apologize." No longer intimidated by the sheep, I waved my arms again and lunged at the ewes, sending them forward. Luke didn't respond.

After several failed attempts, Mandy said, "Well, he's what, ten months old? And he still needs to gain confidence. Try him again when he's a year."

The subdued walk back to my truck took an eternity. To say I was disappointed would be like calling an ocean wet. Frizzle seemed to feel the mood and led the way with her tail down and ears flat.

"Really, don't let him get you down. Occasionally, I've had a dog whose instincts didn't show until they were a year old. Bring him back in the spring. He's had a rough start and is still insecure. He has the pedigree, so we'll see if it wakes up." Mandy handed me a VHS tape. "This is about what we do here, and it shows several dogs working. It will help you see the different stages of training a dog goes through."

After getting a drink, Luke was all too happy to jump back in the truck.

That same silent frown showed for an instant on Mandy's face. Then she smiled and said, "See you in the spring."

On the way home, I had a stern talk with myself. Okay, I had a loving husband, a profession I had worked years for, and a wonderful daughter. A herding dog might just be an unreachable dream. Maybe I was wrong to buy an untrained dog. Or maybe Mandy was right and Luke's instincts would awaken when he was a year old. The logical pros and cons rolled back and forth like marbles in a shoebox until I pulled into the ranch parking lot.

Instead of jumping right down when I opened the back door, my dog stood on the seat and looked at me. I gazed into his sweet, sweet face and wrapped my arms around him. My hands enveloped silky fur, my cheek brushed his neck, and I could feel his heartbeat. A realization washed over me at the speed of pouring honey.

Sometime, long, long ago I had wanted that feeling in my arms so strongly, so profoundly, so completely that I had made a horrible mistake that others had paid for. My hand went instinctively to the jagged scar on my forehead and suddenly I was five years old again.

"My, aren't you a brave one, and so tiny, too," said the doctor. "Let me sit you up here and see what's behind that cloth you're gripping so desperately."

Trembling, I nodded. Blood had saturated the dish towel I held to my forehead—so much blood that it had run down to pool in the bend of my elbow and all over my new yellow Sunday dress. The room and the bright lights swam around me. My vision dimmed, and my five-year-old mind worried that my brain might be falling down my arm along with the blood. I looked past the doctor at the stern face of my father, Sergeant First Class Robert L. Wedding, U.S. Army.

With the movement, my vision focused, and I gazed into the kind, dark brown eyes of the military hospital doctor.

"How many fingers am I holding up?" he asked.

"Two," I said timidly. *Surely, if he's a doctor, he can count to two*, I thought. Then I looked once again at my father standing behind him. I mentally pleaded that he'd notice how I hadn't cried.

My father was not a tall man. He stood five foot eight, but to me he was a giant, always erect, his movements robotic. With a tone that could command steel to bend, he never had to tell me to do anything twice. Our eyes were the same sky blue, and our hair was the color of fall wheat.

"What's your name?" asked the doctor as he took the cloth from my hand.

"Naomi Wedding." My voice sounded shaky.

His fingers gently lifted the matted hair from my face. His bushy black eyebrows reminded me of caterpillars as he frowned. He inhaled, then said, "The lacerations on your legs don't seem too deep. The one on your head concerns me. You might have a scar."

"Serves her right," my father said. "She knew not to go into the chicken pen. That rooster paid the price for her disobedience. Now she can pay it too."

Paid the price... How do you punish a rooster? I wondered, remembering how the bird had flopped around on the ground after someone had jerked him off my head.

"Sit right here," the doctor said. "I'll get the nurse to clean you up so we'll know if you need stitches." He and my father left the room.

What my father had said was true. I had known not to enter my grandmother Elsie's chicken pen alone. She kept around fifty chickens and sold eggs to supplement her income. Often, she would let me be the harvesting assistant when she gathered eggs. She always warned me about Apollo, her prized but crotchety rooster, and the sire of most of the hens in her care.

A blond nurse in a starched white uniform and a funny white hat walked into the room. "Hi, I'm Linda. What's this white stuff?" she asked as she gently dabbed my knee with a tangy-smelling orange liquid.

"Chicken poop," I said. "I fell in lots of it."

The nurse smiled. "I heard you tangled with a rooster. Girl versus fowl… I don't see many of those in here."

Her smile helped me relax, and I giggled, picturing myself in a white shirt with Mighty Mouse's big red *M* on the front.

When all the dried chicken debris had been cleaned from my legs and forehead, she laid me down on a table and covered me with a green paper sheet.

The bright lights above made my head swim again. Then a second green paper covered my eyes, leaving only my head exposed. I watched as two shadows moved above me.

"You're one lucky little girl," said Linda. "That rooster could have blinded you."

I didn't feel lucky. What were stitches? Did doctors have sewing machines? Were they special head machines? Did it hurt? My chest felt like tennis balls bounced inside my ribs. I held on to the table with a death grip.

"This will be a little prick," the doctor said. "It will numb your head."

"Sir," my father said from some far corner. "She needs to learn responsibility and the consequences of her actions. Don't use that local."

"But, Sergeant," the doctor protested. "She's so young." The doctor's hand tensed on my arm. He turned to face the direction of my father's voice.

"She is my daughter, sir." I have the final say. Do not numb her head."

The doctor growled something under his breath as he patted my shoulder.

The sound of metal on metal clinked near my head. My eyes darted wildly, not understanding what it all meant.

Cold hands slipped under the paper sheet to gently hold the sides of my head, and I relaxed a little. Then, all at once, those same hands turned into a vice grip. A white-hot pain like I had never experienced before pierced my head.

"Mommy," I shouted and sobbed. "Mommy, please make them stop."

It did... for a moment.

"Proceed, Doctor," said my father. "You, young lady, had better cease your childish wailing. Your mother is in the waiting room with your brothers. She can't interfere."

But as hard as I tried, I couldn't quit screaming. I felt the excruciating pierce of my skin and the feeling of being pulled during every one of the seven stitches in my forehead.

When it was finally over, we rode home in silence.

"Now you have caused your grandmother to lose her favorite rooster," said my father as we walked into our living room.

I drew in a breath and held it. I knew my grandmother loved Apollo, and he was gone because of me. But I also knew what would happen if my father saw me cry. I kept blinking to hold back the tears.

"Furthermore," He stalked closer and loomed above me, "you acted entirely unbecomingly. Go to your room. I'll deal with you later."

Once in my room, I took off the bloody, dirty yellow Sunday dress, folded it, and laid it in a chair. The torn and stained matching socks could no longer be worn, so I used them to wipe the grime off my white patent leather shoes. My legs had quit burning, and I welcomed the softness of my favorite pink kitten pajamas.

The sound of the razor strap slapping my father's hand rang down the hall. I squeezed my eyes shut and clutched a pillow, expecting to hear the door knob turn.

But it didn't. Instead, I heard my mother say, voice shaking, "Leave her alone," then again, stronger, "I said, leave her alone. She's been through enough. You'll touch her over my dead body."

The next sounds were of a door slamming and muffled shouts.

Darkness covered the room like a shroud when I turned off the bedside lamp. My head hurt too badly to lie down, so I sat with my legs folded up under my chin.

I couldn't believe how quickly the day had turned horrible. It was supposed to be wonderful. Mr. Murry, Grandma's neighbor, had invited me over to play with his Border Collie's five puppies. I'd been too excited and taken a shortcut through the chicken pen to get to the fence separating the properties. If it hadn't been for the horrible, shrieking rooster that attacked me inside the pen, clawing his way up my body, I could have had a wonderful afternoon with the puppies. I fell asleep holding my tattered Felix the Cat. With him, I could imagine how silky the puppies' fur would have been.

The sound of tires crunching over gravel brought me back to the present.

Sharon pulled into the driveway. "Forgot my jacket," she said, coming around her car. She glanced at me hugging Luke. "Well, are you two official sheep herders?" She stopped, her face turning serious. "What happened? Somebody die or something?"

I let go of Luke's neck and shook off the rooster memory. "No one died, and no, we aren't official anything. He didn't seem to have any interest in the sheep, only their poop." I flashed her a forced smile. "Mandy said sometimes they're a year old before their instincts kick in, so I'm not worried."

Sharon placed her hands on her hips. "Aren't you just full of shit and sugar. You might think you believe that, but you didn't tell your face. Hurt's written all over it."

At the typical Sharon comment, I flashed a genuine smile. "Come on, handsome, you can get out."

Leaping down, Luke barked at Sharon and ran to the backyard to pee on a post.

I told Sharon, "Really, I'm okay. A little disappointed is all." I pointed to the haystack. "There's your jacket."

As I watched her pull out of the drive, I looked down at the dog by my side and said, "You are the one I've always longed for, and you aren't a mistake. You can't be."

Chapter Ten

Several weeks later, under a clear blue sky, the jingle-clank-whirr of the manure spreader accompanied the sound of tires crunching over frozen bluestem grass. My cheeks tingled in the cool air. I inhaled the homey smell of woodsmoke from the neighbor's fireplace. Luke bounded ahead of the tractor as if clearing a path. He reminded me of the escort cars with the lights on top that lead the way for an oversized-load hauler.

My dog had added another element to my contemplative manure-spreading time in the hay meadow. He reached a little part of me that felt unfettered, unconditional joy and love. He awakened a place in my soul that I hadn't known was there.

"What is it about you?" I asked as he sped by the tractor. "Why did I make a commitment to you sight unseen? Why did I defy my own rule of always buying a trained animal for a beginning competitor?"

I had always loved my animals. Bobbie Jo held a special space in my heart. But Luke was undeniably different. "Why am I so committed to you... and to herding?"

Just as I spoke the question, a shiver ran up my spine, a feeling that someone was watching us. As I crested the top of a hill, I stopped the tractor and looked around. Nothing. I wiggled in my seat, trying to shake the feeling, but it persisted like an itch on my back I couldn't reach.

Then, I locked eyes with the same coyote in the exact spot under the willow on the pond dam. I caught my breath. "Are you stalking me?" She simply stared, and I sensed no malice or ill intent.

Luke arched around the meadow and came to investigate. My heart clambered around in my chest. I turned off the tractor, got down, and stood on the ground, ready to interfere if that stalker coyote came after my dog.

The coyote's eyes were now intent on Luke. Slowly, the mottled, thin critter rose and slunk to the right.

I tensed. Should I call Luke to me? Would he listen? Then, something happened that took my breath away.

Luke crouched low to the ground. When the coyote moved, Luke matched the animal's steps with stealth and precision.

The scene playing out in front of me held me transfixed. It was more than Luke's herding posture. Something else was happening, something important. Suddenly, I recognized what it was. Luke was staring down the coyote. No, not staring. It was called the "strong eye." My dog was exhibiting not only the physical movements of it but the irrefutable confidence and power.

"Oh, you beautiful boy." My words broke the link between them, and in the next instant, the coyote ran along the pond dam and into the neighbor's pasture.

"Luke, here!" I shouted.

Luke glanced toward me, back to the coyote, then ran to me.

"You have it! I knew it! You have the posture. You have the eye." I rubbed him all over and hopped up and down on the frosty ground.

Luke bounced on his front paws and ran around me as if we were dancing in a tiny world all our own. I dropped to one knee. "Okay, friend, now you need to apply that awesome ability to sheep. I don't think there are many coyote herding competitions."

Half an hour later, I parked the tractor and spreader in the barn. The small front door of the barn opened, and someone shouted, "Hello?"

Luke took off barking.

"It's me, the woman who helped birth you," Peggy said in a cooing tone. "I'm here four days a week, and still you bark."

Luke's hair stood straight up on his back. He circled Peggy a few times. When she didn't make a move toward him, he stopped behind her and sniffed her hand.

As if her stillness had flipped a mental switch, Luke finally stood in front of her with his tail wagging.

"That's my cue." She bent down, hugged him, and rubbed him all over. "You think he'll always do that?"

"Looks like it," I replied, shaking my head. "He stays in the truck when I go to the feed store. The intensity of his barking scares people if they approach him or walk around a corner in his direction. Luckily, my customers here are used to it and know what to do to put him at ease."

"I know he means no harm." Giving him a last pat, Peggy stood and took in a deep breath. "Smells good in here, like earth and wood. Sharon must have cleaned already." She glanced toward the stalls. "I want to ride Maestro if you haven't yet."

"No, he was next. Go get him and I'll help you get saddled."

Knowing the routine, Luke went to his crate.

I latched his door. One of Mandy's rules (that I did follow) was to not let him run free while the horses were moving about.

After walking her Morgan horse to the saddling station, Peggy unfastened the leg and belly straps of his blanket. Both Peggy and I had to stand on our tiptoes to slip the winter wear over the horse's head.

Peggy ran her hand over Maestro's coat. "When we take the blanket off, it's like an unveiling. He shines like raven feathers."

"He's a handsome guy." I ran a curry over his body.

Peggy fetched his saddle and bridle.

"Guess what happened today," I said. "Luke stared down a coyote in herding pose. It's about time to take him back to Mandy's for another sheep session. I bet he's great this time."

"Really?" Peggy peered over Maestro's wither. "Well, I hope you're right."

"You know, now that I think of it," I said, "that's the third time I've seen that coyote out in the day. I get the feeling he's stalking me. And the night Stan first mentioned he knew someone with herding dogs, there were coyotes caterwauling so loudly it spooked Wynonna... Weird, huh?"

"It is weird. Maybe the furry creature is trying to tell you something. Too bad you don't have an animal telepathic link." Peggy chuckled, and said, "Hey, Mrs. Stalker Coyote, what's on your mind?"

My brush stopped in mid-stroke. A chill ran over me. I had felt that animal. I had sensed her eyes following me, and I knew she meant Luke no harm.

I shivered. *Had that coyote come to give me hope?*

Chapter Eleven

A few weeks after the coyote incident, I was hanging up my insulated coveralls in the mud room after Luke and I finished the ten o'clock barn chores.

Mac met me at the door as I entered the kitchen. "Is she with you?" he asked.

"Who?"

"My pig-partner." Mac waved a small stuffed pink pig missing an eye and an ear, one of Bobbie Jo's favorite toys.

"She didn't go out with us." I glanced around the large open space that was our kitchen and living room. "Are you sure she's not in here?"

He squealed, "Pig, pig, pig," in a playful, high-pitched tone, then shook his head. "Bobbie and I play squealy-fetch-pig every night. If she were in here, she would have come running."

From the beginning, Luke had instinctively followed Bobbie Jo's two inflexible laws: do not touch my food or my pink pig. Tonight, he sat looking at Bobbie Jo's full food bowl.

"She didn't eat her dinner. That's not good." I fended off dreaded thoughts of owls, bobcats, and coyotes. Keeping my voice as nonchalant as I could muster, I said, "She probably slipped into the barn when I left the door open. I bet I've locked her in the tack room." Quickly, I slipped a coat on. Luke and I took off for the barn.

"Hold on a second, I'll go with you," Mac called after me.

Bootsie Myrtle climbed down from her bed on the hay and stretched as I burst into the dark barn.

"Bootsie, is Bobbie in here?" I asked.

After searching the tack room and barn, we grabbed two flashlights and trudged through the tall grass to the pond. Like a desperate chant, we called, "Bobbie Jo are you out here? Bobbie Jo." Relief and fear mingled as we found no signs of a wet white Shih Tzu caught in the ink-black crevices made by the rocks and water.

Growing more desperate with each passing second, we went back to the house. The moment we entered the back door Luke's ears pricked up. The dog took off for our spare bedroom and stuck his nose under the bed.

"Here she is." The short-lived happiness at finding her turned to utter dread as I held her trembling body in my arms. I understood instantly that what Luke had heard had been whimpers of pain. "Get a blanket," I called to Mac.

My husband read the panic in my eyes and instantly found a small blanket and his keys. Without a word, in less than a minute, we were on the road to the Animal Emergency Clinic in Tulsa.

The drive felt surreal. The streetlights along the highway blurred together. I held the wrapped bundle of fur baby against my chest, her head cradled by my neck. Her hot, dry nose rested next to my ear. A tiny whimper escaped from Bobbie Jo, and her body shuddered in more intense pain. "Honey, you have to drive faster," I pleaded.

It didn't matter. Hours later, after a panicked conversation with a surgeon that involved the words "clostridium infection" and "eaten away at her bowels," our precious dog left us.

We drove home in shock, poor Bobbie Jo in a cardboard box on my lap.

"What just happened?" I asked. "How can this be real?" I tried to wrap my head around the fact that she was gone, but nothing made sense. I kept seeing her running for the pink pig and bringing it to Mac. I felt her warm body cradled in my arms, safe and protected.

But she wasn't safe and protected. I had let something awful happen to her.

"How did she get it?" I asked Mac. "Did we do something wrong? My Lord, how did we not know she was so sick? She didn't play as much this afternoon, but I didn't think anything of it."

An hour later, Mac and I collapsed into bed, stared at the ceiling, and held hands.

"She was only three years old," I said. "She's been ripped from us. There's a hole in my soul."

"I know... mine too."

We chose a resting place for our girl behind the pond dam. The spot lay nestled in a park-like area framed by cedar trees.

The January day was chilly and clear. Twelve of us—clients, friends, and family—all stood under a clear blue sky.

"Look," Sharon said, and pointed to the upper hay meadow.

Seven horses stood above us like silent sentinels in a perfect row, their heads held high, in respect and reverence.

Encouraged by their presence, I recited the prayer I had written:

MOTHER EARTH, WE RETURN TO YOU THE BODY OF OUR
    LOVED ONE.
HER SPIRIT REMAINS WITHIN OUR HEARTS.
WE WILL ALWAYSE BE GRATEFUL TO BOBBIE JO FOR ALL HER
    LOVE, JOY, AND COMPANIONSHIP.
IN THE MEASURE OF TIME, IT WAS TOO SHORT.
IN THE MEASURE OF LOVE, SHE IS ENDLESS.
WE ASK ALL THE SPIRITS OF NATURE TO ASSIST IN THE
    HEALING OF OUR HEARTS.
WE KNOW THAT THE ANIMAL KINGDOM IS EMBRACING HER
    PRECIOUS SOUL.
AH-HO

Mac placed the pink pig alongside Bobbie Jo.

Luke looked at the pig, then at Mac. Then he tilted his head in a way that made it seem as if he understood. He understood that neither form would play again.

I knelt and wrapped my arms around Luke's neck, burying my face in his silky fur. I felt a stirring deep down below the numbness that had gotten me through the past several hours. Every life is precious, and it is so important to stop and appreciate every moment with your loved ones, because in the next instant, they could be gone.

As our solemn procession walked around the pond toward the barn, I glanced up at the hay meadow. The horses had dispersed and were grazing. A rustling sound drew my attention to the willow tree. Trotting away, brown bushy tail held low, was the coyote.

Chapter Twelve

I n our front yard, fragrant white blossoms from the two aristocrat pear trees danced in the wind and floated to the ground. Deep red velvet mantles adorned the redbud trees that lined the drive. After I groomed the horses, the rubber mats in the saddling stations lay under a coating of horse hair in sorrel, chestnut, black, and gray. Signs of spring were all over the ranch, including the backseat of my truck.

"Look at this," I said to Luke, as I let him out. "I think there's more black-and-white hair on this seat cover than on your body. No, wait, it's all over the floor in the house, too." I shook my head and brushed hair from my nose, then gave him an ear rub.

Mac drove up, parked, and walked over to Luke and me. He bent and peered around my hand as I unfastened the Velcro strap on the seat cover.

"There's something lodged under there," he said, and rummaged around under the cover. "It's a VHS tape. The label says 'Mandy's Performance Dogs.'"

"Oh, yeah, I wondered where that went. Let's watch it after dinner. Maybe I'll learn something."

Later, Mac went into the bedroom that also served as an office to catch up on paperwork,

I inserted the video into the VHS player and curled up on the sofa. In moments, the dance of woman, dogs, and sheep held me captive.

Without a doubt, I knew it was more than simply a desire to be part of that dance; there was a piece of my soul that depended on it.

Mandy explained each level of training while different dogs worked. I couldn't take my eyes off the fluid movement and the obedience of the dogs.

Toward the end of the tape, Mandy said, "Even working dogs need playtime."

I unfolded my legs and moved to the edge of the sofa to call out, "Mac, come and look at this dog. Hurry, before it's over!"

"Just a minute, I'm in the middle of something."

Instantly, I grabbed the remote and stopped the tape.

As soon as Mac stood by the sofa, I pushed Play. A Border Collie with long auburn fur leapt five feet into the air, spun one-hundred-eighty degrees, caught a Frisbee, and returned it to Mandy. The dog's magnificent coat shimmered in the breeze. In the next scene, the same dog circled a small group of sheep, lying down and moving to the right and left on verbal commands.

"She works and plays," I said. "Isn't she gorgeous? She's one of Mandy's youngest dogs."

Mac sat down on the sofa. "That's the first red Border Collie I've seen. She's cool."

"Look at this one." I reversed the tape to find a petite, short-haired black-and-white dog. "He's small, but look at him move those cows around. They respect him. And this one." I fast-forwarded to a dog that looked a lot like Luke. "She's going to a Florida golf course to be a geese control dog."

With his thumb and forefinger, Mac turned my face toward his and kissed my forehead. "I haven't seen you so enthusiastic about anything since Bobbie Jo passed. Why don't you call that lady and take Luke for another lesson? He's old enough now." He grinned. "I don't see any coyotes to work there, but, hey, maybe sheep will do."

I sighed. "I've been a little sullen, huh?"

"I didn't want to say anything because I understand, but I miss her too."

Mac's smile hit me like a warm gust of summer heat. I realized I had been so wrapped up in my loss that I had all but ignored my husband's feelings. A sickly, fluttering stab of pain went through me. "I'm sorry."

"No need to be sorry, but I would like my wife back."

"You're right." I reached down and gave Luke a pat and told him, "Daddy's right. It's time to start your training."

Luke stood, put his chin on my knee, and wagged his tail.

"See, he agrees," Mac said, then tilted his head and wagged an eyebrow at me. "But if you want to erase some of the finer points of your bad behavior, you could make us a baked apple."

With a chuckle, I went to the kitchen to wash, core, and slice two apples. After placing the fruit in small pottery dishes, I sprinkled them with cinnamon. During their thirty-minute baking time, I phoned Mandy.

"Can you put some of that caramel sauce on top when they're done?" Mac called from the living room.

A few minutes later, he closed his eyes and softly moaned as he chewed the apple slice covered with rich, warm caramel.

"Mandy said she has three very quiet ewes she would sell me so Luke and I can practice at home," I said.

Mac came out of his caramel-apple haze.

"Forty dollars each," I said before he could ask.

"That's one twenty," he said. "I suppose I get to build a pen and some kind of shelter?"

I smiled, batted my eyelashes, and nodded.

He shook his head, blew out a breath, and smiled back.

"We go a week from next Thursday," I said.

When Thursday finally arrived, I secured the horse trailer to my truck.

Sharon walked up as I finished. With her fists firmly planted on her hips she said, "So, you're off to buy sheep for a dog. Seems a little backwards to me. Can you make money with sheep or are they just large eating, pooping dog toys?"

I opened the door for my dog. "I'm doing this for the sport of it, not to make money. Luke, here, load-up."

He jumped in.

Closing the door, I turned to Sharon. "Horse competition pays the bills. Herding is something fun for us." I gestured from Luke to myself.

"Just so I don't have to take care of the smelly things." Sharon's voice grew in intensity. "That's not in my job description. There isn't a water faucet by that pen Mac built, so you'll have to carry buckets out there. I already have two jobs, you know."

Sharon's face looked drawn and tense. She always voiced her opinions, but this reaction seemed a little overboard. Suddenly, I noticed her left forearm.

"What's happened to your arm?" I asked.

Sharon held up her wounded limb showing a bandage that came from my horse supplies. The overlarge gauze pad and purple vet-wrap almost covered the orange Betadine solution. "I cut it on a knife in the dishwater."

"Well, take care of it. And I'll take care of the sheep."

Although Luke still traveled in the backseat, a crate was now fastened in the truck bed with bungee cords. His crate and bed would provide a resting place, if needed.

Just before I turned down Mandy's drive, I looked at Luke's reflection in the rearview mirror and said, "Okay, handsome, we start First Grade in sheepherding today. Last time was orientation. Now you know what the campus and classroom look like and what tools you have. We met our teacher, who's very nice. I know you're the smartest, coolest dog to ever look at a sheep. We're going to learn together and have a great time. Got it?"

Mandy was standing in the same spot as before with Frizzle at her side. She motioned me to a different parking spot.

I barely had room to park. As soon as I stopped the truck, Luke bounded out and headed straight for Frizzle, sniffing curiously around her with bright eyes and lolling tongue. "Well, Mandy said. "He sure is more confident." She scratched behind his ears and examined his fur. "Has he grown, too?"

"I'm just happy there isn't urine on my leg." I laughed.

"We'll work the St. Croix I pulled for you. They're in the pen you passed coming in."

Frizzle took that as her cue and bounced along ahead of us down the drive.

Thirty sheep stood in the dry lot across from the round pen. The acrid scent of their urine met us as we walked down the gravel driveway, our shoes making crunching sounds. The sky was crystal blue with the temperature just cool enough to need long sleeves.

Mandy gestured at the three sheep—one white, one brown, and one brown-and-black brindle. "These ladies have been worked some, but not so much that they run to you when they see your dog."

Mandy opened the gate. "They're shedding. Hair's all over the fence."

"Aw, they're sweet." I watched them move just out of Mandy's reach. "Should I groom them to help them shed faster?"

Laughing, Mandy replied, "Don't make them pets. If you handle them too much, they'll automatically run to you. Then, there would be no need for a dog." My instructor grew serious. "Really. Without a challenge the dogs don't learn."

"Got it," I said. *So many rules.* I sighed and decided to do what I had been instructed to do. Luke sleeping by my bed, however, would never change no matter what she said.

As Mandy left the pen, Luke and I entered it. The sheep milled around, alert to the fact that a dog had entered.

Mandy stood on a platform outside the fence. "Take off the leash. Let's see what he does. These girls are fresh from the pasture. They will be easier for him to move than the last ones. If he has a natural balance, he'll walk or run to the other side. Don't freak out if he crashes through the middle. He's just finding the twelve o'clock position. No matter where you move, once he settles down, he'll stay in balance across from you."

Blowing out a breath, I realized how calm I felt. I unhooked Luke's leash.

Luke glanced briefly at the animals but continued following every step I made.

"Most working dogs are either drivers or gatherers," Mandy called. "Border Collies are primarily gatherers. Back away from the sheep, and he should try to keep them with you."

Unfortunately, no one had given Luke the program. He put his nose down to smell poop, then walked through the sheep to me.

"Keep walking. Keep them moving," Mandy called.

I walked, hopped, clapped, chased, and whistled while ewes ran in every direction.

Luke went to the corner and watched his mom work sheep.

Mandy opened the gate. "You two come out. I'm going to get another dog. He's so interested in what you're doing this isn't working. Maybe another dog will ignite the spark."

A few minutes later, she returned with a small, short-coated, black-and-white Border Collie. "This is Jack." Mandy ran her hand down his back. "He gets along well working in twos, so he should be able to get your dog motivated."

As they entered the pen, Jack was aware of the sheep but stayed at Mandy's side.

Quietly, she said, "Jack, go-by." The dog slowly moved clockwise between the fence and the sheep, bringing them to the middle. That put the animals between Mandy and Jack. When Mandy moved right, Jack moved left. If she backed up, he stepped forward to push the sheep toward her. Jack stayed in a twelve o'clock position no matter which direction Mandy moved.

"So, that's balance," I said. "Do all herding dogs have it?"

"Most all gathering dogs do it instinctively, but sometimes balance can be taught." She looked at me, then at Luke, who sat beside me. "The dog has to have some instinct or interest in the livestock, though."

"Are the dogs usually that quiet?" I asked. "He moves so softly the sheep aren't rattled at all."

Mandy ran her hand through her long blond hair. "Jack's had years of training. Most young dogs are way too quick. Their enthusiasm can overload their brains sometimes."

"Enthusiasm, huh?" I roughed Luke behind the ears. "Where do we get some of that?"

"Bring him in and let him go. Jack should get him interested."

Mandy directed Jack back and forth and up and down for at least ten minutes while Luke lay in the shade.

With each passing moment of Luke's indifference, my chest grew tighter and tighter. Bits of logic in my mind told me it didn't matter. Luke had become my beloved companion, and that was all that was important. But deep inside my heart I knew we were meant to work together.

As a last resort, I left the pen and hid, in case I was a distraction. Nothing worked. He simply wasn't interested in moving animals around.

"Well... I don't know what else to try," Mandy finally said. "Jack, that'll do. Here." The small dog stopped mid-stride and walked to Mandy.

This wasn't anything to cry over, but I felt raw, as if I had reopened a wound. With an enormous effort to hold back tears, I said, "Okay then, I can't bring out what's not there or change him to fit my needs. He'll be my barn-buddy."

I snapped on Luke's leash, and we walked up the gravel drive toward my truck.

Something screamed in my mind, *No, no, you can't leave like this. It can't be final. You can't give up your dream.* Then, an image of one of the dogs on the video flashed across my vision.

"Do you still have the red dog?" I suddenly asked.

Mandy paused, looking confused. "Morgan?"

"If she was the one playing Frisbee and working."

"Yes, that was Morgan. I still have her."

I mentally gripped myself and said, "Can I see her in person? Watch her work, if it's not too much trouble?"

Mandy jerked her head toward me as if I had just asked her to juggle monkeys. "Well, yes, but Morgan is very high-energy, and she's only just begun her livestock training. She's by no means a trained competition dog."

All I could see in my mind was a beautiful, playful animal. An animal I knew had an instinct for herding. I had to channel my thoughts away from loss. My entire body felt strung tight, like the slightest quiver would break me apart. "Do you have a dog that's further along in their training?"

As if Mandy could sense I was barely holding it together, she smiled, but her expression held regret. "No, they've all been sold. I only have Jack, and I can't part with him. He's my cattle dog. You need a trained dog, Naomi, a dog that knows what to do. Morgan shows promise, but she's not proven."

When we approached my truck, I said, "Would you get her? I would at least like to see what she can do."

Mandy sighed. "Okay, get your crate and put it under the oak tree. That way your dog will be out of the sun while he waits. I'll be back with Morgan."

After Luke had a drink of water, I hugged him. "It's okay, handsome, you're still my best."

Unlike Jack, Morgan accompanied Mandy on a leash. She kept eyeing Frizzle, clearly wanting to play.

While we walked back down the drive to the round pen, Mandy said, "You've seen the up, down, and recall commands she knows from the tape. She worked a little this morning, so she shouldn't be too fresh."

The moment Morgan approached the pen and saw the sheep, she pulled on the leash and hopped on her front paws.

"She does have balance." Mandy unsnapped the leash, and Morgan went straight to the back of the sheep. All four animals were at the woman's feet in a flash.

After a few short, frenzied minutes, the animals had changed direction so many times my head was spinning watching them. All the while, Morgan instantly obeyed Mandy's calm authoritative demeanor.

"Morgan, that'll do. Here to me," Mandy said. The dog stopped moving forward and ran to the woman.

"Wow, she listened and responded so well," I observed in awe. "That must be what you meant by 'biddable' the first time we talked. It all happened so fast, that was the only thing I recognized."

"She's coming along nicely so far, but she's a lot of dog."

Clouds had moved in, bringing with them a chilly breeze. I knelt to look in Morgan's face and ran my fingers through her full white mane. "You are as beautiful as I remember from the tape. You're smart and talented, too. Would you like to go home with Luke and me? We can be a two-dog family again."

Morgan seemed happy enough to get my attention, but her eyes never left the sheep for long.

Standing, I asked, "How much do you want for her?"

"Morgan is a rare color, biddable, and very well-bred. I've priced her at fifteen hundred."

I sucked in a breath and blew it out. It felt as if she'd said one million. Some part of me knew it was reasonable, but we didn't have that kind of money. "Let me make a phone call."

Mandy clicked Morgan's leash on, and we walked down the drive.

"Look, you saw how fast she is. The only reason I would consider selling her to you is that you do have a training background. You'll need a lot of outside help. Make your phone call. I'll put her in a kennel for now."

My hands shook, and my heart shifted from despair to excitement so fast I didn't know what to feel. I waved my hands in front of my face and forced my mind to settle and think.

Mac was a conservative, logic-driven man. With my cell phone in my hand, my mind arranged all the reasons we should find a way to purchase this new dog. She was beautiful, biddable, and well pedigreed. He would love the well-pedigreed part.

I waited until my hands ceased shaking and I felt in total control before I dialed the number.

"Hi," said my husband's happy voice. "How are my two sheep-herding stars?"

Abruptly, and to my astonishment, my calm logic vanished. "Luke won't work." The words came out in a garbled sob that caused my chest to convulse.

"What? The only word I understood was 'Luke.' Honey, are you okay? Slow down, catch your breath, and talk so I can understand you."

Within a matter of seconds, I had become a crying, hiccupping mess with so much snot running from my nose I couldn't speak. After a desperate, fruitless glance around my truck, I wiped my nose, lips, and chin with my shirt sleeve. "Luke has no interest in working. None. Nada. Zip."

"Well then... don't buy the sheep," was his calm response.

"You don't understand. I want to buy Morgan."

"No, I don't understand. What's a Morgan?"

"Morgan is the red dog we watched on the video. I saw her work today, and I want to buy her." My tears hadn't been a ploy to get my husband's approval or help with the money. I simply couldn't stop them flowing.

"Hold on." I rummaged through my glove compartment for a Kleenex, then blew my nose. "I didn't mean to cry at you."

"Are you better now?"

"I think so."

"I take it Luke is okay, just not interested in working? Well, he's your buddy. Tell me about this Morgan."

As all of Morgan's attributes came tumbling out, my flood of emotions ebbed to a manageable tide. "She has such a pedigree, she's definitely worth the price."

Silence.

Mac finally asked. "Well... how much?"

"Fifteen hundred dollars."

Then there was more silence, a very, very long silence. My heart hammered in my ears.

"How are you going to cover this magnificent canine?"

What an odd question, I thought. "Well, it's not that cold. She has a really thick coat, so I don't think she needs a cover."

A cough on the other end of the line almost blew the phone away from my ear.

"I meant," Mac said in slow, clipped, carefully enunciated words. "How are you going to pay for her?"

"Oh, um… well, that is a problem." I had hoped he wouldn't ask that. I had no idea how I was going to and suddenly, like a flash, it hit me. I shouted into the phone, "We got our income tax money back!"

"That's for a new kitchen floor."

I collapsed against the back of the truck seat. "I know." The possibility of not going home with Morgan seized up my throat, and I whispered, "Please."

Gripping the phone, I waited desperately to hear my husband's decision.

Chapter Thirteen

Twenty minutes later, Mandy jumped down from the truck bed after she said her goodbyes to the lovely auburn-coated dog she had raised.

Luke was in his place in the backseat. It had taken Jack all of three minutes, with the assistance of a barking Frizzle, to load the sheep into the trailer.

"Morgan has never been in a house or inside a truck," Mandy said. "You can do as you wish, of course, but I suggest you keep her routine. Remember, she's a working dog. I think you had a good beginning with her today. I suggest weekly lessons once you've had time to get to know her."

She paused, glanced toward her house, and walked in that direction. "I just thought of something," she said over her shoulder. "Be right back."

The sun cast a crimson glow through the trees as I leaned against my truck. After all the emotional upheaval, I felt peaceful. Purchasing Morgan was the right thing to do.

All the sobbing had been my soul crying out in protest. What exactly it was protesting, I wasn't certain.

Had I been wrong in purchasing Luke for something as important as my herding companion? No, I felt too connected to him. He had bounded into my heart like no other.

Was it the loss of my long-awaited dream? Maybe. Or maybe I was still so raw from losing Bobbie Jo that my heart couldn't take another disappointment.

All I knew for sure was that something about my world had righted itself.

Mandy returned with a piece of yellow plastic. "It will soon be time to learn whistle commands." The object resembled a very small taco with a hole on top. "It will take you a while to make legible sounds. Practice in your truck when you don't have a dog with you."

A similar whistle of metal hung from a lanyard around her neck. She put it in her mouth and made a wolf whistle sound. "That means counterclockwise." Then she blew a bobwhite sound. "That means clockwise." Last, she made a long blast. "That's down. Teaching Morgan whistle commands was my next step. If you can make them correctly when you come back, I'll show you how to teach her."

A huge smile crossed my face. "My first herding whistle. Thank you so much." I handed her a check. "This is much bigger than what I thought I was going to write today."

"Thank you." Mandy hesitated, pursing her lips and narrowing her eyes.

"You're going to miss her. I'll take good care of her."

The woman's jaw tensed and she looked down, clearly holding something back.

I tensed too. What could I have done or said so wrong in the last two minutes? Or maybe she was having second thoughts. Maybe she'd decided I shouldn't have her lovely dog.

For a few moments, her silence sent nervous tremors through my body.

Mandy squared her shoulders. Her intense brown eyes hardened.

"Okay. I'm just going to say it. You're not going to like it, but I have to."

My heart pounded in my ears. *She's handing my check back, climbing into the truck bed, and getting her dog.* The thought came blasting though my mind like fireworks.

"You should put that dog down."

"What? What dog?" I whipped my head around, astonished at her words.

Mandy pointed toward my backseat.

"You're crazy!" I retorted before I could stop it. "There's no way."

Mandy crossed her arms and backed against my truck. "You're attached to him, I know. But you've talked about his incessant barking at people he knows. That could easily turn into fear-biting. And… there's a code, a way of doing business we all adhere to. Charlie Cameron wouldn't want a dog like him anywhere around the herding community. He's worked too long developing a proven pedigree with his imported dogs to taint it now."

By the time Mandy finished speaking, I was shaking with fury. "There's a lot I don't know about the herding community, but no one is harming Luke. I can't believe you even said that."

With teeth bared, a menacing growl came from Frizzle, and the gray-and-black hair rose on her tiny back.

Her attempt at fearsomeness made me smile as she pinned me with one blue eye and one brown eye.

The heated intensity of the moment cooled. I let out the breath I'd been holding. "Look, there might be someplace in my mind where I could understand what you're saying. But there would never be a time I would agree." I folded my arms and set my jaw. "Luke's my buddy, and he'll remain that way."

"The alternative would be to have him neutered. Don't take him to any kind of herding competition and never, ever tell anyone where he came from."

A part of me wanted to throttle the woman. A part of me admired her cool composure and dedication to her beliefs, skewed as I felt they were. Through my emotional rollercoaster of a day, she had been soft-spoken, direct, and understanding.

As much as I didn't want it to be true, Luke had no interest in working. I might have been beyond disappointed, but I could never see him as flawed in any way. "I'll give some thought to what you're saying." From somewhere, I found a pensive smile. "Thank you, thank you for Morgan."

In a few moments I was on my way home with two dogs, three St. Croix sheep, and an empty bank account.

Without a doubt, one of the most disgusting smells in the world is dog diarrhea. I held my breath as I cleaned up Morgan's second bout from the worn vinyl kitchen floor. When the dog upchucked her dinner, it was all I could do not to allow the contents of my stomach to follow suit. For a nauseous moment, the decision to purchase this dog instead of a new tile floor felt like insanity.

"Your very expensive dog is not adjusting very well." Mac held the plastic bag open while I discarded soiled paper towels.

"Mandy said Morgan has never been in a house. I guess we'd better try the kennel."

"Luke hadn't been in a house either, but this didn't happen." Mac tied off the plastic bag and set it by the back door. "He just smelled really bad. Do all the dogs you bring home have an aroma issue?"

My eyes closed as I frowned at him and shook my head. "Let's take her to the kennel."

The panicked look left Morgan's eyes, and she lay down the moment I closed the gate. The Taj Mahkennel Mac had built for Luke was now Morgan's home.

After all the animals had been tended to—horses, sheep, cat, and dogs—we sat down to our own dinner.

"I should get some Good Husband points for thinking far enough ahead enough to pick up pizza," Mac said, talking with his mouth full.

"Honey, you get Good Husband points for the entire day!"

Later, when we lay in bed, he squeezed my hand and said, "We can get a new floor next year." I squeezed back and smiled in the dark.

The next morning as I threw hay into the horse stalls, I kept thinking about what Mandy had said about pedigree lines, integrity, and the world of working dogs being different. I was so distracted, Wynonna Belle's breakfast landed on her back.

"Oops. Sorry, love."

By the time everyone had crunched their bluestem, I felt cold with dread. I knelt to pet Luke and looked into his human-like eyes, and a realization dawned. I knew it didn't matter now, but the thought still crushed my heart. I sprinted to the phone at the front of the barn and dialed Charlie's number.

"Well, hi," said that resonate deep voice I knew so well. "How are you and that dog?"

"Hi, Charlie. Luke and I are fine."

I told him about my day at Mandy's and about purchasing Morgan. Then I said, "I have a question. There's something I need to know."

"I'm sorry my pup isn't working out. I was afraid he was too shy. But fire away, what can I help with?"

"If I hadn't taken Luke, or if I'd sent him back, would he have been put down?"

A hollow silence told me the answer.

Charlie cleared his throat. "At his age, if I hadn't found him a home, yes, I would have had no other choice. Do you want me to take him back?"

"Oh God, no!"

"Look, Naomi, before you come out of your skin, let me explain. A rancher can't afford to feed, provide veterinary care, or spend time with an animal that doesn't have a job. I don't have many that don't have the instincts, and I do make every effort to place the ones that don't.

Experience has shown me that if I place a working temperament in a home and they don't have a job, it results in destructive behavior and angry people. Often, I get them back anyway, so I've just delayed the inevitable."

Even though he spoke in his honey-soft voice, his words still felt like arrows.

Luke would have been put down.

"Okay, I just needed to know. That must be why I knew I had to have him. He'll be my barn assistant."

"All I ask is that you have him neutered and don't take him when you go with your new dog. Have a good time with her. I'm glad you found an animal that will work for you."

After Charlie and I said our goodbyes, I sat and pondered what he had said. The same was true in the horse world. Livestock, working, and competition animals were an investment and needed to show a return.

In my world, our animals were our partners, not a means to an end. I held to the firm belief that every life is precious and should be respected as such. My mind and heart conflicted with our commerce-driven world.

Chapter Fourteen

A gunshot blasted through the clear April morning, and a redtailed hawk streaked upward from the cedar trees. Bootsie Myrtle bolted from her riding place on the tractor and ran for the barn. I jumped straight up out of my seat.

After I stopped and lowered the throttle on the engine, I could hear an angry voice shouting, "I said, Get outta here!"

Morgan had joined Luke that morning as my manure-spreading escort service. I stood up and surveyed the meadow, but no dogs were in sight. "Oh no," I shouted, and gunned the tractor toward my neighbor's pasture.

As soon as I got the tractor stopped, I bolted for the fence line toward cattle chaos. Luke ran back and forth along the pipe-and-cable barrier. His high-pitched whining pierced the air. Morgan was running amuck through my neighbor's mama cows and new calves. The cows were bawling, and the calves were sprinting in every direction with my dog nipping at their legs.

"I'm sorry, Mr. Garrett," I cried out as I ran toward my dog.

"You'd better get that dog outta here," he thundered. "She's either going to run a calf into the fence or one of those mama cows is going to stomp her. She hurts one of my calves, and I'll shoot her."

Mr. Garrett stood with his shotgun on one hip and his hand on the other. His square-jawed face shone like a red beacon. A dirty tan ball cap covered his short red hair.

In the next instant, sheer terror flooded through me swift and horrible. Just as he predicted, a calf darted off from its mother and headed straight for a hog wire fence on the other side of the pasture. Morgan barked and took off after the brown-and-white calf, biting at its tail and heels.

Mr. Garrett raised his shotgun to his shoulder.

"Morgan!" I shouted. "No!" When the dog ignored me, I froze. This couldn't be happening.

The next words came out automatically. "Morgan, down." The raw sound rasped through my throat like sandpaper.

Morgan halted in midstride, crouched on the ground, and looked from me to the wide-eyed, panting calf.

"Morgan, that'll do. Here," I croaked.

With great relief, I realized the hours spent with her and the sheep in my indoor arena had paid off. The dog gave one longing glance at the calf, jumped up, and ran to me.

I grabbed her collar.

"It's a good thing they were heading toward my house," Mr. Garrett growled. "I couldn't risk the shot, or that dog would be dead."

I swallowed before I could get the words out. "This is the first time I've let her run in the pasture. I won't allow it again. I'm so sorry. I hope none of the cattle were hurt."

Once the threat had been removed, the cattle settled down.

Mr. Garrett visibly relaxed and inspected each cow and its offspring. "Doesn't look like any harm done. But keep her at home."

I didn't doubt for a second that he would have shot my beautiful Morgan.

"Yes, sir. She worked cattle where she came from. I didn't think about her being drawn to them here."

To my surprise, a slight smile crossed Mr. Garret's face. His brown eyes lit up the freckles across his weathered skin. "My pa always used dogs to help with the cattle. That dog responded when you used the right words. Makes me think of him and the time he spent with those Blue Healers of his."

"I should have known better," I said. "She goes after anything that moves."

"Never had no trouble with the black one." The man pointed across the fence at the still-agitated Luke. "Keep them both at home."

"Yes, sir." I glanced down at my red dog and ran my hand down her back. "Morgan, come." I walked her across our pasture to her kennel. Her eyes blazed with the fun she'd just had. "Ah, sweetie, my stupidity almost got us into a lot of trouble."

Morgan responded to her fur being stroked as a form of positive reinforcement, but repelled any other signs of affection, like hugs. The only time I had held her face to mine, she nipped at my nose.

In the days that followed, our family developed a routine. Luke and Morgan played in the backyard in the mornings. In the evenings, Mac and Morgan played Frisbee. Luke got excited when Morgan ran after the disk, but then looked at me as if to ask, "Why would I want that piece of plastic?"

The sheep—now named Sue, Mabel, and Sally—were let out to graze during the day. The sweet ewes always stayed between the pond and barn, amid the plentiful Bermuda. Around dinnertime, they were happy to follow my grain bucket into the indoor arena. Mac, Luke, and Bootsie Myrtle would sit in the corner while I did the working exercises Mandy had taught me.

The skyline view on the west side of our property showed no human touch. At sunset, one side of the vast expanse of our world seemed to span to the other. The huge red ball made its descent behind long strands of cumulus clouds, creating vivid hues of magenta, gold, orange, and yellow across the sky.

A grain bucket for the sheep sat on my left side, and Luke sat on my right. As I stood in the giant doorway at the back of the barn, I took in a deep, deep breath. Beauty and peace seeped into my very soul. Our earth was wrapped as a splendid gift. My life here on the ranch, with my loved ones was a blessing beyond measure. I instinctively reached down to stroke Luke's head.

He wasn't there. He had moved in total silence.

"Luke?" I glanced down the barn aisle. "Luke?" He wasn't in the indoor arena. I gazed once more into the sunset and was surprised to see the sheep moving toward the barn. When the three ewes made a slight turn around a boulder, there he was, walking slowly, with his belly close to the ground and his nose out. My boy was moving with the quiet, confident power that I had noticed with Mandy's dog, Jack.

The hair stood straight up on my arms. A single silent tear fell to my cheek, triggering many more. Finally, my brain engaged, and I ran to open the pasture gate.

Once the animals were through, Luke halted in a crouch, eyes on the sheep, and waited until I opened the arena gate. As if in practiced motion, he rose and walked quietly behind them until all three animals stood in the arena.

After I closed the gate, Luke ran to me with, "Here they are, Mom," written all over his face and wagging tail.

I dropped to my knees on the dirt and hugged him to me. I couldn't speak.

"What are you doing down there?" Mac said from outside the gate. "Are you hurt? Is Luke hurt?" Fear tinged his voice as he entered the arena.

"No." Standing, I waved my hands in front of my eyes. "Luke brought the sheep in."

"What? He did? How?"

A feeling of giddiness came over me. "He whistled, and they all came running," I said.

"What?"

"Oh, honey, he went to the pond all by himself, got behind the sheep, and brought them right in here like a pro."

The last remnants of daylight cast a yellow glow through the arena. Particles of dust flitted through the light.

Mac held my cheek in his palm and wiped the dirt and tear stains from under my eyes. "Well, it's about time." A generous smile crossed his face, and he reached down to rough Luke's mane. "Can you do it again?"

My hands shook and my heart did the rumba as Luke responded to every command. I had assumed Luke had been content just lying by Mac while Morgan worked, but, in fact, he had been listening and learning. Within a few moments, I realized Luke was more fluid, soft, and easy to handle. He was more an extension of myself than a separate entity.

Later, I was still glowing in surreal happiness as I turned down the bed comforter. Could it truly be that after all this time and disappointment, Luke's instincts had emerged?

"You'd better put extra covers on the bed," Mac said, climbing between the sheets. "You might float right off. What did you do, flip a sheep-working switch on your dog?"

"I don't know. He was with me one minute, and the next he was gone. I looked all around the barn before I glanced outside. There he was in that splendid sunset, bringing in the sheep. It felt as if it had been planned and painted by something divine, just for us. I'll never forget it."

"Let's hope he keeps it up," Mac said. "He barks at anyone coming around a corner and is still very shy. If you do get to compete with him, your audience might have to watch from the parking lot."

With a chuckle, I snuggled next to him. "We'll know soon enough. One gift at a time."

Chapter Fifteen

L uke joined the nightly sheep-working routine. The differences in the two dogs' working abilities soon became apparent.

Morgan moved the sheep by running at them, as if she had to make them respond.

Luke moved the sheep with his posture and eyes, as if he expected them to respond. In a very short time, we were outside working in the pasture.

Morgan was extremely biddable and energetic. Often, she reacted more quickly than my brain functioned. In her exuberance, she gave Sally a severe bite to the leg and drove Mabel into the pond. I decided to put Morgan's training on hold. I didn't want to create habits with her that would have to be redirected later.

Peggy and I were riding in the outdoor arena one morning when Sharon arrived. Earlier, I had ridden, rinsed, and left a client's English pleasure horse tied in the saddling station to dry.

On Sharon's way to the turnout pens with the horse, she stopped to say, "There was a message on the recorder. That lady you take the dogs to says there's a herding clinic. One of the Border Collie Herding Association judges is teaching."

I trotted Red, one of Peggy's horses, over to Sharon. "Really? When, where?"

"I wrote down the number to call. I think next month."

Peggy rode up on Maestro and said, "Wow, a herding clinic where you can watch other dogs work."

"I haven't made it back to Mandy's in a while, so maybe I could get help with Morgan." My brows furrowed. "But…I don't want to look stupid in public."

"How could you pass up learning from someone who trials and judges? You know that seeing a performance from a judge's perspective can be very helpful." Peggy tucked a lock of red hair under her ball cap.

"Yeah," Sharon declared. "You should go, for sure. I bet he has more than three sheep and"—she pointed toward the pond at my grazing ewes—"I don't think he names them. They're livestock, an investment to make money." She laughed and shook her tangled curls.

I chuckled. "I know. I shouldn't have made them pets. Maybe I'll call and see what levels of training the man is teaching."

Later that day, I paced circles in front of the barn phone. *Do I call or not?* The question bounced back and forth like a Ping-Pong ball in my head. I needed more time with my dogs before I went anywhere public with them. But how could I pass up such an opportunity?

On her way to her car, Sharon stopped in mid-stride as she recognized her note about the clinic in my hand. "What are you doing?"

"Thinking. I do that sometimes before I act."

As she opened the car door, the insufferable woman threw me a look that said, *scaredy-cat.*

Chris, the event coordinator, answered the phone on the first ring. "There'll be classes for the very beginner to the advanced," he said in response to my questions. "Bart Bromstead has years of sheepherding knowledge. Even if you only sit in the stands and audit, you'll learn something."

"I have one dog that I know will work, even though she's a lot for me to handle. But my other dog… I'm just unsure."

I had made a promise to Charlie that I wouldn't take Luke to an event like this. Briefly, I explained my dilemma to Chris. "So, if Luke runs and hides, I would be betraying someone's trust. Not only that, but I would feel really silly."

"I see." Chris was silent for a moment. "If the dog were mine, I would bring him. If anyone can utilize a dog's talent, it's Bart. In fact, I wouldn't want to miss the opportunity to give my dog every chance to make it."

His comment pricked my heart with a stab of truth. I glanced at the backyard where Morgan and Luke were lying in the sun. Both my dogs deserved to receive the best training possible.

Then, a realization surfaced that made my stomach turn sideways. Was my ego behind my first instinct to avoid the clinic? Was I afraid I might be embarrassed?

This clinic could expand my training capabilities and let me move forward with my dogs. The thought of letting my ego make fear-based decisions instead of heart-based or logical ones took my breath away. How often had I unknowingly done that very thing? How many opportunities had I missed?

I asked, "Can I reserve two spots with a credit card?"

"You sure can," Chris said. "I'm ready when you are."

Apprehension about the clinic must have lingered in my subconscious. The night before the event, I dreamt that Luke and I stood in a circus ring. We were surrounded by dozens of wooly white sheep wearing silver sparkly hats and bright blue plumes. Luke wore a black cowboy hat, white shirt, and bow-tie. The long-legged sheep loped circles around the ring and jumped through hoops. Thousands of people occupied row upon row of spectator seats. When I reached down for the ringmaster's whistle, I was completely naked from the waist up.

The alarm jolted me awake at 3:30 a.m. Shivering in horror, I sat up and immediately glanced beside the bed. "Oh, thank goodness," I breathed, waiting for my heart rate to slow down.

"Thank goodness for what?" Mac raked his fingers through his hair and rose to get dressed.

"Luke... has fur."

"Okay," Mac said, frowning and shaking his head. "Let's get you on your way."

While loading Morgan into her crate in the back of the truck, brilliant stars broke through the darkness and the night bugs did their dance.

"This feels weird—Morgan back here and Luke in the truck."

"Honey," Mac said. "You're finding out Mandy was right in how to care for Morgan. Unless you want an aromatic repeat of every time you've brought her in the house, she's fine where she is. You have a three-hour drive. Better get on the road."

Our destination was near Springfield, Missouri. As I drove, the sun peeked over the horizon to announce the arrival of a new day. With it came a heart flutter of excitement. Mandy's instructions ran through my mind: where to place my body, what to do with my hands.

There were still problems, though. For one, my dogs didn't know whistle commands. More spit erupted out of the yellow piece of plastic than distinguishable sounds. I had purchased a shepherd's crook. Holding the blue-handled aluminum tool made me feel very authentic and shepherd-like, but I had no idea how to use it.

Singer Boz Skaggs's voice blasted from the radio. I finished singing the last verse to Luke when I saw the Bart Bromstead Herding Clinic sign hanging from a black-pipe fence. A second sign a mile down indicated I should turn right.

The long driveway was paved with asphalt and lined with black-pipe fence. Dairy cattle were grazing on the right. Two Border Collies and a man were in the pasture on the left, along with a herd of white sheep.

As soon as I stopped at the entrance, a heavy-set man with a big smile approached the truck. His appearance reminded me of an unmade bed. "Welcome," he said and pointed to my left. "You can park over there. The sign-in desk is in front of the hay barn."

He must have gotten up at the same time I did, I thought as I followed his directions.

Suddenly, Luke whined and bounced his paws on the window.

The two dogs I had seen in the pasture were directing a small herd of sheep across the drive right in front of us. They reminded me of school crossing guards. At the direction of their handler, the dogs took the sheep to a holding pen beside the barn. Luke became more excited as the sheep let out plaintive bleats to their friends left behind in the pasture.

"He's eager to go," the man said. "You two should have a good time today." Then he noticed Morgan in the back. "She's a beauty." He tapped the roof of the truck. "All three of you have a good time."

"Thank you. I'm sure we will." Turning left took me to a pasture that served as a parking lot.

Disbelief that I was actually there blended with awe as I sat with a white-knuckled grip on my steering wheel. Around me stood twenty pickups with dog crates in their backs. Some crates were plastic like mine. Most were elaborate aluminum, while a few were multi-compartment trailers pulled by the trucks. People of all ages worked at some kind of dog-arranging—moving crates to shady spots, walking dogs, fetching water.

If this had been an equine clinic, I would have known exactly what to do. I would have been confidently arranging my equipment and prepping my animals. But as it was, all I felt was lost.

Once my dogs had been walked and watered and were resting in their crates, I went to the sign-in table. I felt a little trepidation— well, a lot of trepidation. Would Luke's harmless bark frighten people? Would I be dishonoring Charlie if Luke cowered in the corner? What if Morgan took a bite out of someone's sheep or ran them through the fence? Had dogs ever been expelled from a clinic for tearing a hole in a sheep's leg? Shaking my head, I channeled my thoughts in a more positive direction. It was time to put my big-girl britches on and handle whatever happened.

"Naomi McDonald," I said to the man at the table. "My dogs are Luke and Morgan."

"I'm Chris. We talked on the phone. So, you did bring both dogs… Good."

Chris had well-muscled arms and the golden bronze color of someone who worked in the sun. With his blue eyes, blond hair, and square jaw, he had a Viking-like appeal. His easy grin went right along with his black-and-white T-shirt, which read "Border Collies Have More Fun."

"This is the working schedule." He handed me a piece of paper. "Each dog will work for twenty minutes, once in the morning and once in the afternoon. I have a dog in the beginner class also, so I'll see you over there." He pointed toward the round pen.

His comment stopped me mid-smile. "Wait, you can't be a beginner." Something in the pit of my stomach rolled over as a dreaded understanding flickered.

His next words sent my flicker into a full-grown flame. "Classes are based on the dog's experience, not the handler's." His blue eyes rounded in comprehension. "You're the horse person. You're used to the rider's experience level determining your rank. No, with dogs, it's the animal."

"So, if I compete, it'll be against professional dog trainers and experienced handlers?"

A look of apology on his face, Chris slowly nodded.

I groaned. "Ugh. Boy, do I have a lot to learn. I need to get a handler's rule book."

Luke was eighth on the list for the morning session. I would have an opportunity to watch a few people and their dogs work before we were in the pen in front of everyone.

After checking on my animals, I sat on a bench. The air around me crackled with excited conversation—mostly comments about the fabulous dogs Bart Bromstead raised and trained. He won almost every international herding competition he entered. What had me sitting on the edge of my seat, though, was the comment about how well he coached his student handlers. I wanted to be the best handler for my dogs I could be—compassionate, positive, and knowledgeable.

My entire body was covered in pinpricks as a tall thin man in a white shirt and black cowboy hat entered the round pen. His pale skin contrasted sharply with his manicured black goatee. Bart Bromstead somehow resembled the Luke from my dream. How could that be? Instinctively, I glanced down to make sure I was still wearing my shirt. Something in the way he strode into the arena and stood with a slight slouch reminded me of someone I couldn't place.

"Hello, everyone," he said and flashed a toothy smile. "I'm Bart Bromstead. Are you ready to go to work?"

The clapping audience shouted, "Yes!" My heart shuddered, and I was instantly glad Luke had not been present for the cheering and clapping.

After a few people worked their dogs, I went to retrieve Luke. We walked up as the seventh dog entered the pen, and, with a nod from Mr. Bromstead, the dog's handler unhooked the leash. Her smooth-coated black canine ran directly into the center of the four sheep. The bleating creatures scattered in every direction.

A high-pitched whine erupted from Luke's throat, and he lunged to the end of the leash toward the pen. If I hadn't braced myself on a fence post, I would have face-planted in the shavings and dirt. Then he spun in circles, around and around and around, twisting the leash in a whirlwind. The wrist loop kept him from pulling away as I dragged him in the opposite direction. Once he could no longer see the sheep, he settled and walked quietly beside me back by the haystack.

"My goodness, buddy, you're Jekyll and Hyde. I don't know whether to rev you up or quiet you down." I knelt and ran my hands through his coat, then put his face in my hands. "But we're next, and what will be will be." His human-like eyes seemed to say, *It's okay, Mom. I've got this.* We waited until the handler and dog were gone from the pen before I walked forward and entered.

My legs were Jell-O for the first few steps. Usually, I would be mounted on a horse during a clinic. It felt disconcerting to look out at forty people from eye level.

Luke, however, never noticed the audience. His focus was on the four white creatures that stood quietly at the opposite end of the pen.

"This is Luke," I said with a slight quiver in my voice. "We're very new at this. He's only been interested in working for a couple weeks. He's extremely shy and might run and hide with all of you around. So, I might ask you to observe from the parking lot." The audience laughed. I laughed with them, glad for Mac's one-liner. "But if he does, I'll know that this isn't the place for him."

Mr. Bromstead gave a nod. I released Luke's leash. He was off like a shot behind the sheep, who were pressed firmly against the round pen rail. This made them run around the perimeter instead of coming to me. I moved back and forth in the way that Mandy had taught me, but the sheep were still running the perimeter with Luke behind them.

I felt a tap on my shoulder.

"Do you mind, miss?" Mr. Bromstead said as he grasped my collar and pulled me to the corner, a little rougher than I thought necessary. His narrowed gaze said, "Stay right where you are."

I felt my eyes widen, sucked in a breath, and held it, waiting for Luke's "I'm-going-to-eat-you alive" bark, but it didn't happen.

My dog was so focused on the sheep that he didn't seem to care who else was in the pen with him. The tall man directed him left and right and up and down with perfect responses. When he urged Luke to push between the sheep and fence, however, the dog evaded the man and ran to the other side of the sheep. In the very instant Luke's eyes darted for the second evasion, Mr. Bromstead tapped Luke on the head with his crook so fast I almost didn't register it happening.

Instantly, I covered my eyes with my palms. *Oh, my gargoyles, he didn't just do that*, I internally screamed. *That's the end. I might as well pack up and head home.*

Through my fingers, I saw Luke glance at the man for only a second, then plow right in between the fence and sheep. Soon, he was moving in twelve o'clock balance with Mr. Bromstead and the wooly white animals. The audience clapped, and my ears sang with a rush of blood and excitement.

"Call your dog," said Mr. Bromstead.

"Luke, that'll do. Here."

He stopped and ran to me, tongue lolling, tail wagging, and eyes bright. He reminded me of a child at his first carnival.

The audience applauded again. Someone shouted, "When do we go to the parking lot?"

"That dog's got talent," Mr. Bromstead said.

His words sent a fierce joy to the pit of my stomach that expanded in waves. "Thank you," I gasped. Luke was still vibrating when I attached his leash. As the latch snapped, I thought of the failed working attempts at Mandy's. My hands shook, and a sudden happy dampness filled my eyes.

Luke and I trotted back to my truck and the dog crates. "You were fantastic." I rubbed him all over. "But pee fast, okay? Only one more dog and Morgan goes."

Morgan and I quickly walked back to the pen. She was as eager to work as Luke had been. I felt confident that I could accomplish what Mr. Bromstead had with Luke. But once we were working, that confidence shattered in seconds. My beautiful red dog ran at the sheep, biting at their tails and scattering them in all directions. When she ignored my commands, panic gripped my chest like steel bands.

"Put your body in between the dog and the sheep," Mr. Bromstead said. "Use that crook for something besides an ornament. Block her to the left."

His instructions came fast. But no matter what I did, I couldn't get Morgan under control. The four white sheep bounced off the round pen fences in every direction.

Mr. Bromstead cleared his throat and growled, "We don't need a circus. Call your dog to you."

Did he just say what I thought he did? The word *circus* sent dread careening down my spine. I felt as if I had been exposed as a dog fraud.

Once back at the truck, I knelt and ran my hands through my dog's shining auburn fur. Through a heaving chest and lolling tongue, her eyes shown with excitement. "I let you down. I couldn't keep up with the action in there."

"Now that the fresh has worn off," said a female voice from behind me, "she'll work more quietly. You should get along fine this afternoon." I turned to see a smiling, rather plump, brown-haired woman.

"I was thinking I should pack them up and go home," I said.

"Goodness no, girl. There isn't a one of us that hasn't had the same experience." The woman offered her hand to Morgan, who licked her knuckles. "I hope to see you two after lunch." Then, she walked toward a neighboring truck.

"Thank you," I called out.

In the afternoon session with Luke, I felt the tap on my shoulder and moved aside. The wind had picked up, and bits of pine shavings whirled around. I held my hair out of my face while I stood in amazement at what Mr. Bromstead and Luke accomplished.

Later that day, Morgan was, in fact, calmer and more in control. I left the pen feeling like we had learned something.

After declining dinner out with the participants and Mr. Bromstead, I retreated with my dogs to the hotel room. My body stopped when I collapsed on the bed, but my mind had a recording that kept rewinding and playing what I had learned over and over.

At four in the morning, I awoke to the sound of a retching dog and a floor covered in vomit. Morgan's bout of diarrhea had been silent but no less disgusting. It took all my self-control to not give in to nausea as I crawled around on the bathroom floor cleaning up the mess.

"Morgan, honey, what am I going to do? You can't stay in a crate in the back of my truck all night. Every time I bring you inside, this happens. We'll have to figure something out."

There was no chance of going back to sleep, so I loaded all our belongings into the truck. We were the first to arrive at the clinic grounds. Armed with a large coffee, I sat on my tailgate. Soon, the sounds of tractor engines joined the bleating of sheep and mooing of cattle. In contrast to the previous morning, I walked into each of our morning sessions with hope and excitement.

At lunch, while I fished a convenience store sandwich, an apple, and a bottle of tea out of my ice chest, I heard someone calling my name.

A man with a burgundy Missouri State ball cap shouted, "Naomi, bring your lunch over here."

Someone else echoed, "Yes, come and eat with us." Then the same man scooted to the center of the bench, leaving a vacant seat on the end.

I sat.

The heavy-set brown-haired woman from the previous day asked, "What did you do, stay up and practice all night? You were here when I drove in and both your dogs were good today."

My ears felt hot. "No," I chuckled. "I was bushed, so I stayed in. Very early this morning I had a… difficulty, so I came here. Did you all have a nice dinner?"

"We went for barbecue. It was pretty good, so was the beer. Yesterday was a long day," the Missouri State man said.

A rather thin man in another Border Collies Have More Fun T-shirt said, "You weren't there, so we talked about you."

I peered over my sandwich at him. "Oh?"

"Yeah, or Bart did. He said your black-and-white is one of the most talented young dogs he's seen in a long time." The man grinned.

I held up a finger, chewed quickly, and swallowed. "What? Luke?"

"Yes," said the brown-haired lady.

"Yep," echoed Chris, the event coordinator. "And, to think, you almost didn't bring him. You will never need to hide that dog." He winked.

"Where did he come from?" the Missouri State man asked.

"Charlie Cameron."

Noises of comprehension sounded from all around the table.

"Bet you paid a pretty penny," said the brown-haired woman

"Fifty dollars, actually," I said with a small smile.

The thin man mimicked getting his wallet out. "I'll give you the fifty and raise you a hundred."

With another smile, I shook my head. "There are a lot of nice dogs here. I'm learning tons from Bart and watching all of you. Thank you, guys, for being so welcoming."

By the end of the day, the success with my dogs had me feeling so heady I could have trod on starlight. Two people approached while I was loading crates and supplies.

"Your male dog has talent," Bart Bromstead said. "I'd be interested if you wanted to sell him."

Stunned, I plopped down on my tailgate. What the man had just said was an enormous, unexpected compliment. And about Luke, of all dogs. The afternoon sun glinted around the tall, black-hatted man leaving his face in shadow. He tilted his head as if scrutinizing me. When his black-goateed face moved into the light, gone was the kind dog handler, gone was the efficient clinic facilitator and showman, replaced by... I didn't know what. His brown eyes were hard with hatred—no, condescension, maybe?

I stood up and squared my shoulders. "My dog's not for sale."

He handed me a business card. "Your Luke, I think you called him, is forgiving in nature, so you might be able to fix training mistakes. But in my opinion, it would be a shame to waste such a talented animal." Bart Bromstead strode away.

My mind raced around in absolute befuddlement as I secured the two dog crates in the back of my truck. What was the matter with that man? Did he dislike me, or was I reading too much into a facial expression? Isn't an instructor supposed to be patient and kind to beginners?

My mind ran on. Up until those last two weeks, Luke had shown no interest in herding, but now he was a star. Mandy had all but insisted that I put him down. Charlie had said he would put him down if I hadn't taken him. I had promised to neuter and hide my boy away. But now, this experienced trainer had actually offered to buy my dog.

Just when I thought the weekend could hold no more surprises, another one walked up.

Chris was standing at the back of my truck when I turned around. He pointed toward the picnic table. "Do you have a minute? Can we talk?"

Chapter Sixteen

"I'm sure you're wondering what I want," Chris said, sitting on the picnic bench.

I took the seat across from him. "It's been one surprise after another all weekend."

The scent of freshly mowed hay accompanied the rhythmic purr-clatter of a diesel tractor in the next pasture. The sound brought Mac to mind. He, too, was probably on a tractor, mowing. I needed to get on the road.

"Most of the participants stayed in the same hotel you did. I hope it was okay."

"It was fine."

"Good." Chris shifted on the bench. "You didn't tell us about your red dog's breeding, or where she came from." He rested both elbows on the table.

I felt my eyebrows climb. "Morgan came from Mandy Weis."

"Ah." He nodded. "Mandy has a reputation for breeding nice dogs. I've seen her compete, and she's a pretty good trainer. But her style is different from Bromstead's, as you found out."

"Yes, the man physically pulled me away from my dog. If I hadn't been so excited about the outcome, I would have been horrified."

Chris's eyes narrowed in thought. "I've never seen him do that before. I think it was because he saw the potential in your dog."

"Well, I was dancing around like a goober, clueless on what to do." I huffed out a breath and shook my head.

Chris shrugged and said with a hint of humor, "Aw, we've all been there. You really impressed everyone the second day. You catch on quick. So, I'm sure you noticed the differences in how your two dogs work, didn't you?"

I nodded. Where could this be going? Had I broken some unwritten protocol? Was he making small talk until he worked up the nerve to tell me? He'd mentioned the hotel—had they complained about the smell in my room? I was sure I had cleaned the floor well.

"When your red dog... Morgan, right?" He looked at me for confirmation.

"Yes, her name is Morgan."

"Well, when she's in a tight spot, she runs in and bites."

"Yep." *Obviously*, I wanted to add, but didn't.

Chis gave me a half-smile. "Did you know that unless there are extenuating circumstances, dogs that bite are disqualified?"

Heat climbed up my chest to flush my face. I really needed a rule book. "No, I didn't know."

"So..." He made a circle with his index finger. "In a long, roundabout way, the question I'm leading to is: would you consider selling Morgan to me?"

My body stiffened with shock. "Why Morgan?"

A breeze came up and Chris pushed down on his ball cap. "I need another dog for my dairy in Kansas. She's well-bred and has the right amount of training to go right to work. Your black-and-white has more talent than you can fit in a sack. You don't need Morgan. So, it's a win-win for both of us."

"Oh." I pursed my lips. My jumbled thoughts ran in every direction.

"She can be taught not to bite," Chris continued. "Actually, with stubborn cows, it can be a good thing. But to compete with her, she's going to need... well." He hesitated.

"She needs someone who knows more than I do." I understood.

He nodded.

I thought about the day Morgan went after Mr. Garret's calves. The running and chasing were normal for an unsupervised, untrained enthusiastic dog. The all-out biting should have been a warning. I hadn't known enough to be concerned.

Chris formed a tent with his fingers. "She would strictly be a ranch dog and a companion to the one I already have. From what I see, that might be a better occupation for her."

"There's something you should know about her. She doesn't do well in a house or riding inside a vehicle. Her bodily functions go haywire."

Mandy's and Charlie's faces had held the same expression I now saw on Chris. It seemed to say, "Why would a working dog ever be in a house or inside a truck?"

"My kennels are top-notch and she would live with Ace, my ranch dog. We lost his brother a few weeks ago. He needs a companion, and I need another working dog. Ace would teach her the ropes."

The entire weekend seemed unreal. Disbelief shifted to comprehension as a realization came to the surface. Luke hadn't barked at anyone once, and he hadn't cowered or run in the opposite direction. It was as if the awakening of his natural instincts had brought out a hidden confidence.

Then, Chris's earlier implication that Morgan needed a more advanced trainer hit me like a hammer: cold, hard, and simple. I had no idea what I was doing with either of my dogs. It felt as if I had wasted precious brain space in unnecessary anxiety about Luke. Morgan, my star, the savior of my herding dream, was turning out to be different than expected. I was learning that her quick enthusiasm didn't equal power and confidence.

"Are you okay?" Chris asked. "I hope I didn't offend you. You've been quiet a long time."

I felt tears rising but blinked them back. I would not cry. I would not. "I don't know what the heck I'm doing here. Right now, I'm so out of my element and confused, I don't know which way is up. I couldn't make a competent decision about which socks to wear if I had to."

I blew out a huff of breath, then wondered why Chris was looking intently at my truck.

"Ah, I think I see." He smiled, a warm understanding in his eyes. "Your truck."

"Yes, that's my truck," I replied, confused.

"I don't know many women who drive a one-ton diesel dually around. You said you trained horses for a living. What kind of horse trailer do you pull?"

"A white aluminum four-horse gooseneck." This man was driving me crazy with questions. For the measure of a few heartbeats, I didn't care if he saw the irritated expression cross my face.

He just smiled again. "Okay, your truck has custom pinstriping. I bet your trailer is painted to match?"

I nodded.

"And you have ridden a long time and had years of instruction, and now you're teaching, training, and hauling amateurs and youth riders to shows."

"Yes, that's what I do. Why?"

"Horses can be around eleven hundred pounds, so you are handling huge animals every day. Your rig is the size of many commercial carriers. You have a western profession mostly occupied by men. Yet"—Chris held up a finger—"your dogs were bathed before you came, and both had matching collars and leashes. I would say you're suffering from Queen/Cowboy/Artist-archetype syndrome." He leaned back, crossed his muscled arms behind his head, and took on a self-satisfied look that said, "I hit the nail on the head."

"An arka-what syndrome? What are you talking about?"

"I was a psych major in college. In fact, that's where I met my wife—we were both practicing psychologists for several years. I inherited this place and the one in Kansas, so now I'm a rancher. My wife still practices, though. One of my heroes is Carl Jung. His theories of archetypes helped me understand my patients on so many levels."

"But you didn't tell me what an arka-whatever is."

"An archetype is an unconscious inherited pattern of thought."

"How does that relate to queens and cowboys?"

"There are primary archetypes—king, queen, princess, prostitute, child, victim, nurturer, rescuer, hero, teacher. The list goes on. You're a queen and a shepherd combined. There must be a dose of teacher in your psyche too. These subconscious patterns can influence every decision we make." Chris's eyes crinkled at the corners when he smiled.

"Archetypes can also influence how we react to situations. The Queen/Shepherd in you feeds on authority and leadership—your kingdom must be protected, directed, and nurtured. The artist wants it all beautiful. The horses are your throne, and the cowboy wears spurs. Here"—he waved his hands out wide to encompass the dog clinic—"you're unsure of yourself and your abilities. I would say you haven't felt that way in a long, long time."

As Chris talked, I thought about how uncomfortable I felt looking at the audience from eye level. And I realized I loved the feeling of power that driving into places with my big rig and four horses gave me. Standing in the trainer's box when my students were competing gave me a sense of accomplishment for myself as well as for the student and horse.

"Sorry," Chris said. "I can get carried away."

My face didn't flush this time. It blazed. Angry heat rose from my belly, up my chest, to my cheeks. I thought my ears might turn to flame at any moment.

"Uh-oh." Chris's light expression faded. "I know that look. My wife would have bruised my shins under the table for saying that to you, for interfering." He sighed. "When I noticed your insecurity and how hard you fought the tears earlier, my psyche-rescuer came out."

I tried to swallow, but my throat was too tight and dry. This man, a man I hardly knew, had just cracked me open. He had cracked through my shell like opening a walnut, exposing the bumps and crevices of my emotions.

A frown creased my forehead. "I don't know if I like you more than or less than I did a moment ago." Then, I remembered the night Mac and I discussed the recycling of manure in the earth. It seemed as if the manure in my mind was flying all over again. I chuckled, and the tension in my belly unwound. "I think I got so angry because you're right, and it's something I never would have thought of."

"The quick anger and the flush on your face told me all I needed to know. Your mind can hide emotional triggers from you and me, but your nervous system can't. Is it okay if we do one more thing? I can tell how important herding is to you. Then, I know you need to be on the road."

I sat back and crossed my arms, as if the posture would protect my heart. "Go for it, psyche guy."

Once more, Chris tented his fingers. "Close your eyes and get back on your horse or throne," he smiled. "Whatever is comfortable. Breathe in and think of the feeling you have when a horse responds well, when you've taught them something difficult."

"Okay." I felt silly closing my eyes in front of someone, but I did as he instructed.

My lips formed an involuntary smile. I could see myself stroke Wynonna Belle's neck. I could feel the lovely mare's fluid canter. I could sense her willingness to do what I asked.

"Own that feeling," Chris said. "Let it push out the doubts. Let that feeling push out the insecurity."

I took in a deep, deep breath and nodded.

"Now that you're in that space, in that frame of mind, think of this weekend and describe it to me."

Suddenly, the feeling of accomplishment abandoned me. Doubts and confusion were firmly planted in my heart. My brain felt empty… sad. Frustrated tears threatened me again. "I don't know what you want me to say."

"It's not for me to put thoughts into your mind. I'm just a guide to help you search your own heart. Past events, probably from your childhood, took away your confidence. Hard work and accomplishments gave it back on some level. This weekend has knocked you off your throne, and doubts have replaced your power. The feelings you get from the

Away To Me, My Love

essence of Queen, from self-confidence, from the creative Artist, and from the salty Cowboy are what you were born with."

Ropes of desperation yanked me in every direction. Then, in a rush of dizzying clarity, chills ran up my spine. Words burst out. "I would appreciate my dogs as the enormous gift they are. I would think of this as another adventure and be glad of the experience." I sobbed and caught my breath. "I would be kind to myself. I would believe in myself."

A quick laugh erupted from Chris. "Yes! The transformation in your face is amazing."

"Thank you," I said in barely a whisper.

"Collect your thoughts," he said. "Relax for a while. The kind of work you just did can be way harder than anything physical."

"The archetype theory is interesting," I said. "Wow, it really fit. I never would have thought of myself as any of those things until you mentioned them. I want to know more."

"Jungian teachings are out there. Several people have written about them. I used archetypal patterns for years in my practice to help people identify with themselves. It also helps someone to understand others in their personal relationships."

I stood and walked toward my truck and dogs. Chris strolled up beside me and put a brotherly arm around my shoulders.

"I feel like dancing home," I said.

"If you can't get rid of the skeletons in your closet, at least teach them to dance."

I laughed. "So true."

When we reached the truck, Chris said, "I'm serious about Morgan. After you've had time to talk to your husband and think about it, let me know. Be safe going home."

Morgan jumped onto the tailgate and ran into her crate. "You're ready to get home, aren't you, girl?" Her look said, "Close the door, please, so I can curl up in here," which is exactly what she did.

Luke leapt into the backseat, eyes alight with renewed energy. As I drove down the driveway, he bounded back and forth across the seat. *Look, Mom*, he seemed to say. *There are sheep everywhere.*

I drove in silence for several miles, mystified by the amazing events of the weekend, mystified by the two very different offers for my dogs. Chris, I understood. Maybe he was right—I had known from the moment I had taken her home that Morgan was more aggressive than I felt comfortable training.

But Mr. Bromstead... Had I read too much into his facial expression, his posture? I shivered as the image played through my mind. One thing I knew for sure: Luke would never be for sale.

Chapter Seventeen

A light June rain tap-danced on the metal roof of the barn. One of Peggy's Morgan horses, Red, stood quietly after completing warm-up exercises.

I shifted in the saddle to pat his rump. "Good boy." The rain had brought cooler temperatures, and the moist air felt like heaven on my face and arms. From this vantage point on Red's back, I could see the pond through the opening of the barn's enormous back door. A brilliant rainbow arched from the giant willow trees to the water. The surface danced with red, blue, yellow, and green. On the opposite side of the pond, a cottonwood tree dropped white fluffy bits, like cottony snow in the light rain.

Red's long mane waved slightly in the breeze. "I bet you're liking this air as much as I am, huh?" I asked him. "Let's leave the door open until too much rain comes in."

Red was the only monochromatic horse I had ever seen. He was the same rich color from ear to hoof. His mane, tail, and body shone like polished garnet. At three years old, he was of medium height and gangly.

Training Red was like teaching a sensitive, youthful ballet dancer. The horse easily learned the maneuvers of a reining pattern—spinning, stopping, and speed control. His eagerness to please and sensitivity required me to be extremely subtle in my training requests.

"Time to work on spins," I told the horse as we walked toward the center of the arena.

As I lifted my bridle reins to ask him to rotate to the right, lightning hit the cottonwood tree and a thunderous crack split the air. The skies opened, and a torrent of rain pummeled the roof like giant fists. Wind blew rain into the door opening.

Red leapt three feet straight up into the air, leaving the ground with all four hooves. He landed and instantly performed the spin I had asked him for, spinning on his right hind foot as if to escape the devil himself.

I had been poised for the turn but not the leap, and both my feet came out of the stirrups. With no support under my left leg, sheer momentum sent me careening off his side. I grabbed for the saddle horn, and my right spur hung up on the seat skirting.

Thankfully, the one word Red knew unequivocally was the one I shouted: "Whoa."

He did just that. He stopped so quickly his front legs splayed apart.

Dangling from the horse, I had a good view of the underside of his belly, and I could smell the sandy loam four feet from my nose.

In a conversational tone, to try to keep him calm, I said, "Well, buddy, if I get my spur uncaught, I could dislocate my shoulder when I land on the ground. You might jump on me. If I try to shimmy up your side, I could poke you, which would be very bad."

"Why are you talking to that horse's belly?" shouted Sharon through a chuckle. "He could probably hear you better from on top."

I yelled over the rain noise. "Sharon! I'm glad you're here."

"Me, too. You look funny hanging there."

"I've been dethroned. Please help me unhook my spur. It's caught."

"There's a lady on the phone for you. She says it's about dogs and sheep." Sharon opened the arena gate and walked in. "I hate to leave her hanging, but I'd better take care of your hanging first." She giggled. "And I'll close the back door. You have a pond in the arena."

Sharon's innate calm reflected her time at the racetrack. "It's okay, Red," she crooned softly. "I'll get that crazy woman on the right side of you." She held the reins, stroked his neck with one hand, and released my spur with the other.

With a curling motion, I hit the ground on my back and rolled away from Red, instead of under the horse's legs.

Red did jump again, but Sharon firmly guided the anxious horse in the opposite direction.

Dusting off my backside, I said, "Thanks."

Sharon handed me the reins. "I've been in the same position myself. I'll take a message from the lady on the phone." She slid the back door closed, latched it, and chuckled all the way down the barn aisle.

"This is where the Queen gets back on, Red." My hands shook a little as I grabbed the saddle horn, bounced up, and threw my leg over.

Through the saddle fender, I could feel Red's rapid heartbeat against my calf. His nostrils flared in unison with his pulse. We walked small circles until we both had a normal heart rate.

Sharon had written down the name Colby Ferguson and a phone number. Also drawn on the paper was a fuzzy sheep with a saddle and a stick figure person hanging from the side.

Chuckling, I dialed the number.

"Chris from the herding clinic in Missouri said I should give you a call," Colby said after introductions. "I'm always looking for someone to work sheep with, and he thought you might be interested."

From there, the woman just kept talking about her dogs, her sheep, her horses. She spoke with such a level of animation that I could clearly visualize her hands waving like windmills.

"The lady that took my message said you were having minor horse difficulties. Is everything all right? What kind of horses do you train?"

"Everything is fine." I laughed. "One of the Morgans spooked, and I found myself looking at the underside of his belly. Mostly, I train Quarter Horses, though. I do hunter under saddle, reining, and trail."

"I've ridden jumpers, so I've seen the underside of too many Thoroughbreds." She chuckled. "So, we have horses in common as well as herding."

By the end of the call, we had arrangements for me to take Luke and Morgan to her place in Blackwell, Oklahoma, the following week.

On the big day, Luke ran back and forth on the truck's backseat with an excited whine when he spotted the St. Croix sheep in the two pastures that lined Colby's drive.

"Okay, Mr. Luke, you've gone from disinterested to a sheep-berserk dog. I'll take the berserk anytime. I know you'll listen and be a good boy," I told him, then muttered to myself, "I hope."

Colby came out of a double-wide mobile home. Her brown leather boots echoed loudly as she walked across her redwood deck and down the stairs. She had long blond hair plaited into two braids, bib-coveralls, and a red T-shirt. She also had a large round abdomen indicating she was at least seven months pregnant

Before she reached me, she called out, "It's warm today, so set up your crates under the pecan tree by the four kennels."

Closing the door of my vehicle, I turned full circle, taking in the rich green meadows that encompassed the entire place. "Beautiful!" I pointed toward one of the back pastures at a red metal horse barn trimmed in white with matching flowerpots filled with yellow hibiscus.

Shaking hands, Colby smiled. "I can't tell you how happy I am you came. Chris said your dogs are really nice."

As I lowered the tailgate and jumped into the back of the truck, I said, "I think they're great, but mostly I'm overwhelmed by how much I have to learn." I snapped on Morgan's leash. "Will you hold her while I get her crate down?"

"Hand her here. I'll see if she needs to pee." Colby led Morgan to a grassy area. "You're certainly a pretty girl. Can't wait to see you work."

After my two crates were placed under the tree, I opened the back door, and Luke bounded from the truck.

"Luke, here! Sit!" I shouted. A pungent, musty smell and the plaintive bleats of sheep came from every direction. As Luke spun in circles, he reminded me of my first time at Disneyland. With so much to see, my head felt like it was on a swivel.

Dropping to my knees, I wrapped my arms around him. "Luke, be still." Rising to my feet, I said, "It's never taken a wrestling match to snap a leash on him."

Colby led Morgan to the crate. "Are you as ready to work as your friend over there?" she asked as she stroked the animal's back. "Let me get one of my dogs, and we'll go to the pasture in front of the house." Colby went to the end kennel, opened the gate, and said, "Mike, come."

A dog very similar in appearance to Luke trotted out of the kennel. "Mike, here," Colby ordered, and he walked beside her. "This is my right hand, my go-to guy." She reached down and rubbed behind his ears. "Huh, Mikey?"

During the short walk, I raised my sunglasses to wipe the sweat at my temples, glad I'd changed into shorts and tennis shoes. Then, I glanced around. "There must be... what, a hundred St. Croix here? What came first—do you have sheep for your dogs or dogs for your sheep?"

"Mike came first. I bought him fully trained from Rodger White in Gainesville, Texas. Rodger raises herding dogs and cutting horses. I started out with just a few sheep but soon realized I had to keep changing them to keep Mike interested and sharp. Every time I sold the sheep for new ones, I made money. Now, the sheep are a thriving business for my husband and me. My two young dogs, I'm training myself. How many sheep do you have?"

"Three. Mable, Sue, and Sally."

Colby gave a half-smile and slowly shook her head. "You've named them. I bet they run to you when they see your dog."

I nodded.

"Really tame sheep are good at the very beginning, but soon it backfires. You'll see."

A five-acre pasture sprawled in the front of Colby's house. "This is where we'll work," Colby said. "I put five wethers in here before you came."

"Weathers? Do they forecast rain?" I grinned.

Colby rolled her eyes. "A male sheep with all its equipment, or testicles, is a ram. A castrated ram is a W-E-T-H-E-R," she spelled.

"Okay, a female sheep is a ewe, a male intact sheep is a ram, a no-balls sheep is a wether. Got it," I said.

She pulled a couple of small, sturdy gray bands from her pocket and laughed. "I only keep a couple intact boys. A rutting ram can be mean, and they stink. Their necks and chests get huge with muscles and they... well, ram their heads into anything and anyone. I never put two of the beasts together. They'll butt heads until they're exhausted, or one is crippled."

"What happens to the wethers when they aren't suitable for training dogs any longer?"

"They go to the sale." Colby noticed my grimace. "Oh, lordy, you do have a lot to learn."

"That's where they go to slaughter, huh?"

"Yes. I didn't like it either, but when you can't work them any longer, there's no other place for them. We don't need wandering, eating yard ornaments."

My stomach felt as if something nasty had invaded. I couldn't stand the thought of Mable, Sally, or Sue as a leg of lamb or on a hamburger bun. Shuddering, I directed my mind down a different avenue. "Those wethers"—I pointed to the five sheep in the pasture—"they look pretty big. Will they go to sale soon? How much is one worth?"

"Those guys haven't been worked much, so they'll be here until the fall. Their worth depends on the price per pound, but they should bring about seventy dollars each. I'll have about thirty when the time comes."

"This herding life is much more complicated than I thought." I raked my hair out of my face. "Dogs that aren't suitable for a certain kind of work are put to sleep. They're meant to live outside in kennels. Sheep come and go. Don't make friends with them because they'll end up on someone's plate."

Colby smiled a genuine, compassionate smile. "It's a way of life for the farmers and ranchers who have always provided food for us city folk. You're entering that world."

Luke raked his paw against my leg, as if to say, "We'd better get working, my world is waiting."

"Those boys are in a good place." Colby pointed to the five wethers. "Send your dog when you're ready."

After the clinic, I knew more about body position, the use of my crook, and commands. My confidence had grown enormously. I whispered in Luke's ear as I unsnapped his leash, "Okay, handsome man, let's show Colby what you can do." Rising, I said, "Away to me."

Luke took off from my right side and ran straight for the five grazing animals. Suddenly, two broke away from the others. Luke chased after the one running directly for the pond.

"Luke, down," I yelled. When he ignored me, I stood frozen in a clueless state of panic. The leggy brown wether jumped straight up and landed in the pond, splashing a wave of water four feet into the air.

Never losing focus, Luke did the same. His nose and eyes bobbed gracefully up and down under the water, like a porpoise.

"No," I screeched and sprinted for the pond. I had just met this nice woman, and now my dog was about to drown her wether. I simply couldn't let that happen. When I got close, I bent and took my tennis shoes off. No rain had fallen in Blackwell for the last few months. The level of the pond had receded, exposing gravel and rocks that sliced and bruised my feet, slowing my approach to the water.

"What are you doing? Stop!" shouted Colby as she ran toward the pond.

"Going to get your sheep," I yelled back. "I don't want him hurt or for you to lose seventy dollars."

"Sheep swim! Stop!"

I halted on the edge of the pond. The sight of the bib-coverall-clad pregnant woman running toward me made me laugh.

"So, what do you do to get that animal out? Call him? He doesn't have a name. Can Luke bring him?"

Colby bent over her belly, grabbed her knees, and panted. "Call your dog. Sheep are herd animals."

Down was the command I used when I wanted Luke to stop. "Dow—," I began, then stuttered and stopped. What if Luke sat all the way down in the pond, underwater? Shaking my head, I lowered my voice to a guttural growl and yelled, "Luke, here-to-me now."

To my utter amazement, he did just that. Luke turned away from the bobbing wether and swam toward me, his eyes and nose dipping as he quickly approached the shore.

Balancing on the uneven rocks, I bent to greet him.

My dog stopped on the edge and shook every inch of his body. Water flew in all directions, splattering me with algae and who knew what else.

Rising, I tottered gingerly toward the grass. Luke followed, wagging his tail and spinning. His look said, "Wow, that was fun."

Colby glanced at the shaded corner where her dog lay. "Mike, go-by."

The dog rose and took off clockwise around the four grazing wethers. After a few commands from the woman, the sheep stood at the edge of the pond.

Soon, the waterlogged sheep paddled over to the shore, waded to the rocks, and joined his friends.

"I'm so, so sorry," I said to Colby. "But that was awesome to watch. Mike wasn't even beside you when you directed him. I would have gotten the rights and lefts confused. He followed every command quietly and guided those sheep around the rocks they didn't want to step on."

"It's all in a day's work, believe me," Colby replied. "I've had sheep in worse situations. Your dog came in too close is all."

My hands shook, and my heart seemed to be bouncing from one side of my chest to the other. I winced and held my breath as I put my shoes and socks back on.

The woman and her sheepdog moved to the shaded area.

A feeling of *déjà vu* belonging washed over me. This was all new, but it felt so right. Every maneuver required in a herding competition was an enactment of life on a working ranch: penning, moving from one pasture to another and around obstacles, separating or culling out numbers. It was the same with equine competitions.

Chris's theory on archetypes came to mind. People working in offices, shops, and factories could fulfill their innate need to be ranchers, cowboys, shepherds, and even queens with the preparation and knowledge needed for competition.

"Hey," Colby shouted. "Earth to the woman with the wet dog. Let's get back to work."

Colby had me move in closer to the five wethers. As a result, Luke quickly understood that he had to run out much wider. Following Colby's concise, calm instructions, Luke and I fetched the sheep several times and put them in the pen.

Morgan, however, was a different story. When she ran at the sheep and nipped, Colby couldn't call out fast enough for me to respond and avoid sheep running in every direction.

The woman took over directing Morgan with an agility that didn't seem possible, considering her awkward shape. Colby read every little nuance the sheep made: an ear twitching, the direction of their noses, which sheep the others followed. Soon, Colby had Morgan under control and got the sheep fetched and pinned.

Later, after the dogs had been returned to their crates, we sat on the deck.

Rattling the ice around in her tea, Colby said, "Naomi, your red dog is nice, but..."

My lips pursed. "I know. She's too much for me."

Colby nodded.

"So, I take it Chris told you he offered to buy her?"

Again, Colby nodded.

"Do you think I should sell her?"

Colby set her glass down. "Not for me to say. She's nice, good looking, well-bred. I can see why you bought her. She's doesn't have Luke's eye, innate power, or form. Most importantly, she doesn't have his forgiveness."

The sun had drifted to the other side of the mobile home, leaving the deck in heavenly shade. Nodding, I said, "A forgiving flexible personality is priceless in a dog or a horse."

"I think you see why you need to keep changing sheep. He went in too close and fast at first. Sheep that haven't been worked much will usually split from the herd. He has some bad habits, but look how quickly he changed when you corrected him. He's so biddable and focused that even when you make mistakes—and I say *when* because you will make training mistakes—he will grow with you and learn."

In my mind, I saw the wet, stinky, shaking dog that Charlie had unceremoniously plopped onto the truck bed... The dog I had bought sight-unseen... The dog I had originally built my dreams around, then had those dreams shattered when he showed no interest in working.

I shuddered as I remembered my pity for the terrified animal, my anger at Charlie for his treatment, my fear that I had made a huge mistake. But, most importantly, I relived the instantaneous, irrefutable love I had felt the instant he was cradled in my arms. A sudden warmth expanded my chest. I blew it out in a sigh. "This tea is good. What is it, green and mint?"

"It's sun tea. I use green tea bags and mint from my garden. It's good." Colby put her feet up on an upturned bucket. "You could send Morgan off for training. But even with that, I don't think you'll have a Luke."

"Chris seemed nice. I liked his archetype-psyche stuff. He helped me understand my situation with the dogs. But can he finish her training?"

Smiling, Colby replied, "Yeah, he's a good trainer and takes good care of all his animals. He's helped me with that psyche stuff too. Can't seem to quit, I think he's a"—she put her finger to her lip—"rescuer. Yes, he's a habitual rescuer. Sometimes I think someone needs to rescue that man."

"That's usually the case," I muttered.

"Look, Chris will be here for the cattle trial in Ponca City over the weekend. I have an empty kennel. If you decide to let him buy her, bring her here, and he can take her home when he goes."

Suddenly, something in my heart and mind connected, and I knew without a doubt what I had to do. "I'll leave her with you now," I said before I could change my mind. "Luke and my horse business are my focus. Besides, the money and time I have invested in her was worth it. Working Morgan awakened Luke's instincts, and I can't put a price on that."

Later, I hugged Morgan goodbye. She went directly into the kennel, turned around, and sniffed through the wire at the young dog next door. Then she lay down without so much as a glance toward me. "You'll be happy on Chris's ranch, pretty girl," I whispered. "You'll get along better working cattle. This is the best for all of us."

On my way to the truck, a slight breeze kissed my cheeks. I glanced through the branches of a tree just as a hawk crossed the sky. For a moment, I stood in silence, letting all the small synchronistic messages envelope me. Tears of loss flowed down my cheeks, but I smiled, knowing my beautiful girl would be happy in her new life.

Chapter Eighteen

Two months later while cooking dinner, the phone rang. After noticing the Missouri area code, I punched the speaker button with my knuckle, said, "Hello," and continued chopping onions.

"Morgan proved to be a little harder to control than I thought," Chris said. "One of the mama cows kicked the dog's hip when Morgan charged her calf. It was a couple of days before she could walk, but when she started working again, I had a new Morgan. Now, she works in tandem with my other dog, and they can bring in an entire herd from my south pasture."

I let out the breath I had been holding from the moment he said hello. "Oh good," I said. "I mean, not that she got hurt, but that you're happy with her."

Chris had agreed to bring Morgan back to me if she wasn't useful on his ranch. I would gladly return his money and keep her as a pet rather than let her be put down.

Not only had the call eased my guilt around selling her, it reminded me of our conversation about archetypes. My short, crazy experience with the man had brought a new awareness of subtle things, like quirky parts of my personality and why I felt comfortable in certain surroundings and not in others. We said our goodbyes, and I followed with a little mental thank-you to the man I thought I could be friends with.

"Sounds like Chris is happy with Morgan. That's gotta make you feel better," Mac said as I set a bowl of vegetable soup in front of him.

After taking my place across the table, I watched him intently. "What's up?"

"Huh?"

"Your comment and the look on your face don't match. Your mind is on something else."

"Well, aren't you the detective?" Mac said.

"Call me Sherlock Holmes. Now, you're avoiding my question. Fess up, buddy."

Mac's forced smile faded into a thin grim line. "I can't go to Oklahoma City with you tomorrow. My boss called this afternoon. For the first time in all the years I've been there, he's flying in to review quarterly reports." Raw regret swam in his light blue eyes. "I'm going to miss your and Luke's first sheep trial. I know—I know how important this is to you. I don't want to let you down. I want to be there."

I picked lima beans out of the soup with my spoon and chewed slowly. Before I dove for a carrot, I grinned and said, "That's okay. Peggy said she'd go."

For a few delicious seconds, I observed a myriad of emotions streak across my husband's face: disbelief, relief, a hint of anger, then irritation. The irritation came back and stayed there.

"You're enjoying watching me flounder here! I worried all afternoon for nothing!" Mac's voice rose, then softened. "I wasn't sure what I dreaded more… telling you… or not going with you. You seem to be entertained by my suffering here."

"Maybe." I held my index finger and thumb an eighth of an inch apart. "Look, I appreciate you wanting to be at my first trial. I want you to be there. I'm only smiling because you did what we all do, including me." I placed my hand on my chest. "We worry, dread, or avoid telling someone things that we believe will result in a negative emotion."

I waggled my spoon at him and went on, "So, you could have given me credit for understanding—which I do—credit for knowing you and making a backup plan. It would have spared you worrying about it all afternoon. Furthermore, I know you've supported me through this sheepdog thing, and I appreciate and love you all the more for it."

My husband pointed two fingers into the air, rotated them in a circular motion, said, "Touché," and continued to eat his soup.

The next morning, Mac stood in the doorway of the bedroom, and smiled at me. "You look nice. I like the blue."

"Thanks." I finished buttoning the green-and-blue plaid shirt. The contrasting pocket and cuffs were a small yellow floral print, which gave the otherwise masculine garment a feminine touch.

I turned to model my starched Rocky jeans, polished blue Justin Roper boots, and a hard-earned trophy belt and buckle. "Okay for my first herding trial?"

Mac's approving gaze was all the answer I needed.

"That's a shepherd's look if I've ever seen one," he said, "but there's something missing." Mac opened the top drawer of the dresser and took out a small brown paper bag. "I got this for you. I thought it was better than that yellow plastic thing you carry in your pocket."

I chuckled. "Fancy wrapping." I peered inside the crumpled bag, and suddenly, my hands tingled.

"Here." Mac took the brown paper and removed its contents. "By the look on your face, you'd think I bought you the crown jewels or something." He placed a braided leather lanyard over my head. A shiny, stainless steel dog whistle hung just under my breasts.

"This means more than the crown jewels," I said, and held the small flat whistle reverently to my lips. "This means my dog and I are a working team. This means that no matter what happens today, we made it. Somehow, this feels so right, like the weight of the whistle fills a hole that needed filling. Thank you."

Mac held me to him and kissed the top of my head. "Hey, you don't have to wear a western hat, so that should make you happy. You'd better get your dog. Peggy will be here any minute."

In no time, Peggy, Luke, and I were in my truck. The purr-clatter of the diesel engine sounded more rhythmic than usual. The three of us floated through our two-hour drive to the Oklahoma City Fairgrounds.

The stoplight on Meridian Avenue blinked to green, and I turned left into the fairground's livestock entrance.

"I'm looking forward to meeting Colby," Peggy said. "It's good of her to come today, considering her baby is only a few weeks old."

"I wouldn't be here without her and her sheep. She's had us work young ones, old ones, and everything between in every pasture on her place. I feel certain there won't be any obstacles. I just don't see what could go wrong."

Peggy pointed to the left. "There's the midway, and there's the north arena. Oh good, we're near the ribeye sandwich stand. And there's the frozen fried cheesecake truck!" She patted her tummy and sucked in a breath. "One won't hurt."

A long walk later, we stood in the doorway of an enormous white metal building. I thought my heart might fly from my chest and take to the sky.

"Peggy, it's as if I'm back twenty years." I inhaled deeply. "Smell that sandy loam and diesel."

Without warning, Luke lunged to the end his leash and spun around. I reached down and stroked his back. "You don't see them, but you know those hairy creatures are here."

"We'd better grab a spot as far away from the holding pen and arena as possible," I said. "He'll go berserk if he sees the sheep." We walked down the long alleyway, found a corner tie-up, and set Luke up with a horse-blanket bed, a collapsible water bowl, and a chew.

"Naomi," shouted a familiar voice. Colby approached, minus the tiny passenger she had been carrying around for nine months. "Get signed in while they're setting the arena up. That way you can watch a couple dogs work." She pointed to the opposite end of the building. "The table is over there."

While we walked toward the sign-in table, I tried to introduce Colby and Peggy to each other, but Colby seemed distracted.

The second time she glanced at her gray flip phone, Peggy and I both grinned knowingly at each other.

"First time to leave him?" Peggy asked.

Colby nodded. "Little Steve is with his dad. I'm sure there're okay, but… you know."

"New-mom jitters," I sympathized. "Had them too. But I'm so glad you came. At least I know one herding person here."

"Geez, I'm glad to get out of the house for a while. By the next trial, I'll be ready to bring my dogs."

A short redheaded man stood next to a square folding table by the rear entrance of the building. When he saw us, his eyes lit up, and he walked over to hug Colby.

"Rodger," Colby said as she pulled away from the hug. "This is my friend Naomi, and her friend Peggy."

"Welcome. Glad you're here," he said as he shook our hands. "You're early. I take it you're in the novice class."

I nodded. "Yes, sir."

"What's your dog's name? I'll sign you in and tell you what number you are in the running order."

"Luke."

Rodger glanced about halfway down his sheet of paper and said, "You're eleventh to run, out of twenty-two. We're working Barbados today."

"Barbados!" Colby exclaimed.

"Yep, hauled them in myself from Joe Mitchel's place."

Colby's brows lifted, and her lips turned down in a grimace. "This is Naomi and Luke's first trial."

"Oh." Rodger held his lips in the O so long, my lips involuntarily began to form the same shape.

Then, his mouth snapped shut, as if he were going to say something, but thought better of it.

"This might be a silly question," I said, "but are Barbados a breed of sheep?"

Smiling in unison, Colby and Rodger both said, "Yes, they're sheep."

"It won't be long before the novice class starts," Colby said. "You have plenty of time to see how these sheep react to different dogs. Luke is quick and fast, so Barbados might be a good match for him. One thing about herding, a dog learns to work all kinds of animals."

Just outside one end of the arena, an eight-foot folding table and two chairs stood on a flat-bed trailer. Just inside the arena on the same end was an eight-by-eight-foot portable pen. About fifteen feet away from the pen, the ground was marked with a white X.

As we found seats on the bleachers, a tall man in a black cowboy hat and white shirt stepped onto the flatbed trailer and sat in one of the chairs near the folding table.

"That guy is Bart Bromstead, the judge," Colby said. "They'll begin as soon as the scribe is seated. The white X on the ground is the handler's spot."

I felt like someone had poured ice water over my head. "He's today's judge?" I asked.

"Yes," said Colby. "Oh, that's right. He facilitated the clinic you went to." Then she looked directly into my face. "Why do you look so pale? Did something happen between you two?"

"He… he wanted to buy Luke," I stammered.

"And that's bad because…?" Colby lifted her shoulders.

Letting out a breath, I said, "It wasn't what he said, it was how he said it. When he first made the offer, I thought of it as a compliment. But it didn't take long for his facial expression to convey anything but that. I knew when he walked away that he felt my dog was too good for me."

"Colby's brows furrowed. "I've gone to some of Bart's clinics and competed when he judged. He seemed okay to me."

"Maybe I read too much into his expression or he was tired after the weekend. Anyway, can't do anything about it now. I'm just darned happy to be here."

The first contestant to enter the arena was a young redheaded boy around fifteen years old. By his side was an all-black dog. The pair stood two feet away from the white X. Once the dog had sat quietly beside him, he waved his hand in the air, and a man and dog brought four tall brown and black sheep through the gate at the opposite end.

"So those are Barbados," I said. "They look more like deer on steroids."

"Yeah, they're a hair sheep from Africa. They're more economical to feed and they cost less to begin with, so herding associations favor them. They're as tough as mountain goats."

"Man, they're fast," Peggy exclaimed.

While we were talking, the black dog had run quietly along the fence on the boy's left making a wide arc behind the sheep. Then the dog lay down. As the dog slowly rose to his feet, all four sheep sprinted down the arena as if he had used a cattle prod.

Within seconds, the sheep were twenty yards from the boy, who had moved to the pen and opened the gate. The teenager gave a long blast with his whistle, and the dog dropped his belly to the ground. Three of the sheep plowed directly through the gate. The fourth sheep glanced back at the dog. Without hesitation, the boy used his crook to tap the ground behind the lagging sheep. The animal didn't run into the pen; he leapt into the air and vaulted inside.

"Oh, my goodness!" I gasped. "The entire run took less than two minutes! That boy and dog were phenomenal."

"They should be," Colby laughed. "That's Rodger's son, Carl. He's been herding since he was five. He's as good a handler as his dad."

As realization dawned, I felt my eyes grow round. "The man at the sign-in table is the Rodger who trained your dog, Mike. You bought the two young dogs from him."

Colby nodded. "Although that boy's black dog is a novice as far as competing, he works every day on Rodger's cutting horse ranch. It doesn't seem fair when you're used to the amateurs and professionals being separate divisions in the horse world, but herding is different."

"That rule went down hard when I learned it at the clinic." I sighed and gave a light shrug. "Oh well, I'm not here to win. I'm here to share something fun with Luke. Speaking of my dog, those runs are so fast I'd better go get him ready."

From just outside the building, I heard a female announcer say,

"Katie Donley and Reba entering the arena, Naomi McDonald and Luke on deck."

Maybe he heard his name over the loudspeaker, or maybe he felt my heart pounding against my ribs, but Luke's entire body quivered in anticipation. His human-like eyes lit up in sheer delight, and he hopped on both front feet. I knew at that moment, without a doubt, that he lived for working. His natural instincts, desire, and power had burst forth.

His enthusiasm joined mine, lifting both of us in a whirlwind of giddy joy. "Stop," I had to say to myself. "Breathe. You can't go in there without a brain." I took several deep breaths, did my best to calm my racing heart, and walked inside.

We approached the gate just as Katie and her dog exited.

I bent and held Luke's face in my hands. "This is just like walking into one of Colby's pastures, only smaller. Let's go work some Barbados sheep."

After hanging Luke's leash on the gate, I patted my left leg. "Luke, here." It took about three circles and two lunges forward before he conceded and occupied an area somewhere near my left side.

"Luke, sit." His tail brushed the ground, and he popped back up.

I lowered my voice, trying to sound tough. "Down!" He hit the dirt, swiveling his head in all directions like an owl.

The distant sound of a rollercoaster and the blending of animal and food smells stirred a realization in my belly. I grasped the gift from Mac hanging at my chest, tapped the crook in my right hand, and looked down at the beautiful dog vibrating with anticipation at my feet. A distant memory rose within me. Only this time, I wasn't a spectator. I was in the arena with my whistle, my crook, and my handsome, wonderful dog. Twenty years after that epic visit to the state fair with my friend Ellie, I was actually standing at a handler's post.

A masculine throat coughed and cleared.

The world came back into focus, and I glanced behind me.

"Ma'am, this is a timed event," the judge said, and attempted to sweeten his tone with a smile. Then he tipped his hat with his index finger as a gesture to begin.

"Sorry," I mouthed, and smiled back.

Following the example of previous competitors, I raised my arm to show we were set and ready.

Once the four Barbados were settled at the opposite end of the arena, I glanced down and said, "Go-by." That's when my heart went into overdrive and everything fell to pieces.

Instead of a controlled canter toward the sheep, Luke flew like a dog rocket. I screamed, "Luke, down!"

His belly briefly brushed the ground directly behind the sheep. For a heartbreaking moment, I realized I didn't have a command for "stay down," to make sure Luke didn't lift the sheep until I asked. At Colby's, he had developed his own natural pace.

The four hairy animals broke apart like the sheep were a rack of balls on a pool table and Luke the cue ball. Luke chose the largest wether to chase toward the right fence line.

My brain finally engaged, and I reached for the whistle hanging at my chest. Although the arena was small enough for my voice to carry, Luke responded better to the intensity and tone of a loud blast from the tiny instrument. But I hadn't noticed something vital about the beautiful metal whistle: it was much smaller than my yellow plastic one. The new one fit into my mouth differently, and I couldn't make the air pass through. I blew dollops of spit down my chin instead of the command that would make Luke understand that I really, really meant down.

The wether didn't resemble a sheep so much as it did a gazelle as it leapt straight up and over the five-foot-tall fence.

I was never quite sure if what happened in the next moment was a fortunate or unfortunate incident. Because of Morgan, I knew the no-biting or nipping rule very well.

My dog leapt into the air just as far as the sheep had, latched a mouthful of canine teeth onto the hairy monster's rear leg, and pulled him back into the arena.

Once again, all four Barbados were inside the fencing. They just happened to be scattered to the four corners.

The animals were changing course so quickly my brain couldn't keep up. My dog could, though.

Luke knew his mom wanted those sheep in the pen, and, by golly, they were going to do just that. He took over as soon as I quit attempting to control the chaos. With lightning speed, all four animals were rounded up, as if a giant lasso had appeared from the sky and brought them together.

The instant I realized they were all stampeding directly at me, I sprinted to the eight-foot-by-eight-foot square pen and opened the gate... a second too late. Luke chased them around the enclosure instead of into it. The animals circled the pen twice before I used my crook and body to form a barrier to the side. Luke veered out just enough that the sheep turned right into the opening.

The audience applauded.

It was Luke's and my job to take the sheep out of the pen and back to the holding area. As soon as that had been done, Luke ran to me and sat down. Tongue lolling, eyes shining, his body language said, "I did it, Mom. I got them in." He was the happiest being on the planet, and so was his mom. Laughing, I dropped to the ground and wrapped my arms around him. Then I stood and took a totally undignified, giggling step toward the judge's platform.

The man's soft brown eyes and smile from earlier had vanished. His eyes were cold and hard as black granite. With his goatee-framed lips in a tight line, he growled, "Please save your affections for outside the competition area."

"Yes, sir."

Peggy and Colby met me at the gate.

"How exciting," Peggy said.

"Pretty splashy run," Colby said as she reached down and roughed Luke behind the ears. "I was afraid those sheep would be boogers. But you got them under control, mister."

I tilted my head and smiled at my friend. "You're being kind. It was a sheep-wreck, a really fun sheep-wreck!" Then I glanced at the judge and my stomach plummeted. "Did I do something wrong, break some protocol?" I asked.

Colby shifted her attention from Luke to me. "You do look a little frayed. No, I didn't see anything. It was a little crazy, yes, but nothing wrong as far as arena protocol. You were disqualified for your dog dragging the sheep back into the pen, but that's a rule. Very helpful on a ranch, not so much in a competition arena."

"I don't know herding rules," Peggy interjected. "What makes you think you did anything wrong?"

I frowned. "The judge went from pleasant to hateful, like I'd committed some crime, or kicked his cat. The same thing as at the clinic."

Luke brushed against my leg and looked up.

I sighed again. "Okay, buddy, let's get you a drink. Then a pee break."

"Why don't you two get some lunch and watch the advanced classes?" Colby said. "I have a couple friends to visit. The herding community around here is a nice one, but rather small. I'm sure people want to know who the new girl is."

While my friend and I ate our lunch, my eye kept going to the judge's platform. "Watch that Bart guy, Peggy. What do you see?"

"Well, he's taking his job seriously, eyes always on the dog and sheep, giving the scores to the scribe without hesitation. You know, watching him from here, he seems a little dark and broody, but he smiles and tips that black hat to every contestant. I haven't seen the bogeyman you described."

"Maybe it's just me. I keep trying to figure out if it's something I do when working my dogs... or am I taking someone with a grim-dry personality too seriously?" I took a bite of my sandwich and swallowed. "This is going to sound really silly, but if you put a black cowboy hat and a white shirt on Luke, would my dog look like him?" I pointed at Bart.

Peggy laughed for a second and choked. "Well, he does have a long nose, and with that goatee and white skin, you could say that he resembles a Border Collie. How did you come up with that?"

"Dreamt it… the night before the clinic. I dreamt of a circus with Luke dressed like the judge and sheep running around us. It was a real shocker when he walked into the round pen looking like that. But that's not the really weird part…" I felt my ears heat up. "I was naked from the waist up, like I was being exposed for who I was." I shivered. "Could the dream mean that he will expose me for who I really am?"

"Or," Peggy said, "the sparkly hats and sheep running around means 'have fun,' and the bare chest means don't be afraid to let it all hang out."

Laughing, I said, "I like your version better." I bagged our sandwich wrappers and stood. "Ready?"

"Ready."

"Let's tell Colby thanks and goodbye and head home."

We had just finished loading up when I realized something was missing. "Dang," I muttered as Luke jumped onto the backseat. "The collapsible water bowl isn't with the rest of his stuff." It was too expensive to leave.

"Do you want me to walk back with you to get it?" Peggy asked.

"No, it's a long way. Stay with Luke. I'll hurry."

The number of fairgoers had more than doubled. To get back, I had to skirt children in strollers and people carrying roasted turkey drumsticks, ears of corn, and several species of stuffed animals.

A trailer loaded with the trial equipment had just left the arena, so I took the shorter route across the soft dirt. As I passed through the gate that led to the holding area, I heard two voices, one male and one female. The conversation came from the other side of the bleachers.

"She's a friend of Colby Ferguson's," the female voice said. "Colby said she's a horse trainer."

Thinking the woman must be one Colby's friends, I took a step forward to introduce myself. Then a man spoke, and I halted.

"That's some dog," he said.

Instantly, I recognized the voice as one of the judges, and I waited.

Had he really complimented my dog again? The thought made my stomach do a happy little leap. Maybe I hadn't done anything wrong. Maybe something else had set him on edge.

"A tenacious, bold, but biddable dog," the woman said. "My Bita is the only one I've ever seen jump into the air and bring a sheep down like that. Love to have him in my kennel."

"Aw," I whispered and crossed my hands over my heart.

"Better with you than that dimwit of a woman. It's a shame to see such a nice dog ruined."

What? The words felt like a kick in the gut. For the span of an erratic heartbeat, I simply couldn't breathe, couldn't think. *Dimwit of a woman. Ruin my dog.* The words held me frozen in place.

Behind me, people were leading llamas into the arena and tying them up along the fence railing.

Using the distraction, I made myself take a glance through the bleachers.

The judge leaned on the cement block wall. One foot rested on the wall with a bent knee while the other foot supported his body.

A woman with curly, chin-length salt-and-pepper hair was seated on a large wooden crate. She peered at the man through red glasses. "She's new, and that's a young dog. Give her a break." After a short pause, her face tensed slightly, and she stood and glared up at the tall man. "Goodness, Bart, you shouldn't talk about contestants that way."

Her words must have been lost in delivery, because the man went on speaking. "If she's so new, she should have bought a trained dog. Or, if nothing else, put that one in training with someone that knows how to blow a whistle. Someone who knows a sheep's head from its ass. I can't believe her, strutting around wearing that championship belt buckle like she's some hotshot horse trainer. She should stick with horses if she's that good, or maybe she stole it."

His last statement was what finally made me start moving. But during my third angry step, I thought of Colby. This was her world, her friends. I wanted to be part of it. She had been so good to me. I couldn't just blow up at a judge.

My nerves were a stretched wire, my thoughts twanging. After clenching and unclenching my fists a few times, I walked as casually as I could muster into the holding area. "Oh," I said, and placed my hand on my chest as if startled. "I thought everyone would be gone."

Bart stiffened and stood upright. He lifted his hat and raked his fingers though his hair.

"Left my bowl." I pointed at the blue canvas bowl in the corner. Ignoring Bart, I held my hand out to the woman. "I'm Naomi McDonald."

She shook my hand and smiled sweetly. "Helen Owens, nice to meet you. I'm a friend of Colby's. She's enjoyed working dogs with you for the last few months." She gestured toward the man. "This is Bart Bromstead."

"We met at the herding clinic." I picked up the bowl, which was still half full of water. Until that very moment, I hadn't known how much internal fortitude I possessed. I poured the water into the corner rather than on his boots as I so, so badly wanted to do.

He didn't smile as I spoke, but he did relax his shoulders somewhat.

I forced a grin up at him and said, "I'll remember you always as the judge that's unfamiliar enough with protocol to speak unkindly about contestants to other contestants."

He sucked in a breath, and the cords in his neck stood out. His face instantly suffused red. For a moment, I thought he would strike me.

Helen coughed and put her hand to her mouth, either out of panic or to stifle a chuckle. Whichever it was, she caught Bart's attention.

He looked at Helen, then opened and closed his mouth a few times. Finally, he growled, "Everyone is entitled to their opinions."

"That is so true." I nodded with insincere sweetness. "I couldn't care less about your opinion of me. That's your business."

"Damn straight."

I thought of the same situation happening with one of my new riding students, and how it could profoundly wound a youth. My voice gained strength. "You represent not only the fair board but the herding dog association in an official capacity."

"I do." He took a step toward me and puffed out his chest, reminding me of a threatened rooster. "I judged that mess you made today fairly."

"That's just it," I retorted, unfazed by his stature. "It was *my* mess. My business, not yours."

Helen sat back down on the crate, grinning.

Bart looked stunned. "You were out there in front of everyone."

"Yes, and their opinions of me are their business. They don't represent anyone in an official capacity. Spectators will always have opinions, and they're often not kind." My hands went to my hips. "A judge bad-mouthing a contestant is just... unethical. It carries more weight, and overheard... can be very harmful."

Over the loudspeaker, a man announced that the llama division would soon begin.

"Naomi," Helen said. "We'd better clear the area. And you've given old Bart here something to think about. I hope to see you back again."

"Thank you." I glanced into Bart's hooded eyes. Something dark and painful lingered there. "Well, I can't say I hope to see you around." I found a smile and a shrug. Then I headed toward Peggy and my dog.

During the long walk back to the truck, I had time to think and settle all my frazzled parts: heart, head, nerves. That left me exhausted. I didn't share what happened with Peggy. I hadn't really understood it. What I knew for sure was that overhearing unfair criticism from an official could shatter someone's budding confidence. It might turn them away from competing altogether.

Around ten o'clock the next morning, Sharon came down the barn aisle and began unsaddling the horse I had just ridden. "That dog lady, Colby, is on the phone," she announced.

"Thanks." I walked to the front of the barn where the phone hung on the wall.

Colby launched into her message without saying hello. "Helen called me last night. I hope you didn't let that butthead get to you."

Admittedly, I had stared at the ceiling with my mind turning over and over alternate possibilities for hours—possibilities as to what I could have done differently during our competition, what training methods I needed to change or add. Although the "butthead," as she so aptly called him, had been out of line, he had sent my mind into overdrive. I had examined every word I said, and how I could have handled it more appropriately.

"Hello?" Colby said. "All I hear is birds chirping. Are you still there?"

Her comment made me chuckle. "Oh, the guy rattled me for a while. I wish I'd handled it differently. It's not good to start off with bad feelings. I have to say, though, I've never had an experience like that before."

"Helen was horrified when she realized you heard Bart. She hopes you didn't take it personally. Marsha, the lady who wrote down the scores for Bart, said he had been edgy all afternoon. She thinks you and your dog weren't ready to work flighty Barbados."

"From what I could tell, she's right. But Luke and I can only get better... I hope."

"That run was amazing, I'm proud of the way you hung right in there with all that chaos. You two gathered those crazy sheep from the four corners and got them penned. Rodger ask me if you knew what a talented dog you had, and I told him I didn't think you had an inkling. You simply loved the dog. He felt you did the right thing when you let Luke take over. It showed you were in tune with him and not trying to be macho."

I sighed. "You know, some people think I'm battling giant odds. Some think I'm going to fail, and some think I'm great. I've come to realize that everyone has their own perceptions, but the only ones that count are mine. All I can do is my best with my dog."

"Yeah, that's something I need to keep in mind. By the way, Helen's weaning thirty head of wether Barbados next week. She'll sell you some if you want. Twenty bucks a head is pretty good."

I knew if I wanted to rise to the challenge of working different types of sheep, Luke and I would need to practice with some of our own. When Colby and I ended our conversation, I had Helen's number, and she was my next phone call.

Chapter Nineteen

W hen Helen came out of her house to greet me, I noticed something I hadn't seen yet in my herding travels. A Border Collie exited the house with her. Everyone else had retrieved their working dogs from kennels. *This woman might be someone I can relate to,* I thought.

"This is Bita," Helen said.

"Nice to meet you, Bita." I held out my hand and was nuzzled by a too-warm nose. I glanced up at Helen, who simply gave a weak, solemn smile at my recognition.

Returning the smile, I gave Bita a rub around the collar. "How beautiful you are."

As if she felt the truth of my compliment and had just made a friend, she walked by my side as I looked around.

"This house is wonderful," I said with eyes wide in amazement. The sprawling log dwelling reminded me of a country estate, only this one was constructed of round cedar timbers that had been notched and joined at the corners.

"About half of it was here when we bought the place. The rest, my late husband and I built. It's taken a while for all the logs to age and look uniform. The house is a bit big for just me, but I love it."

"So, you raise cattle and sheep alone?"

"Three years, now. I do have a couple farmhands. One will be mowing here soon." Helen put her hands on her hips and glanced around. "Let's move your truck and trailer to the spot where you'll load the sheep. Pull up by the barn there, then back the trailer at an angle to the front of the drive. There's a long gate we can close to make a chute."

After I parked, Luke and I joined her and walked down the path. The day was a bit chilly. I was glad I'd grabbed my heavy burgundy hoodie.

Two oak trees in front of the barn stood so tall, they appeared more like monuments. Purple ash trees lined the drive down to the pastures and pens. Brown leaves crunched under our feet.

"These Barbados were weaned last week," Helen explained as we strode to the pen. "They've been wethers since they were a couple weeks old." She gestured to the left. "Over there."

My attention had gone to the right. "What are those?" The animals caught my eye and I veered in their direction as if pulled by a magnet. "They look like children's toys more than live animals. Look at those tiny ears." The sheep had white wooly bodies and spindly legs, making them appear to be wearing dresses. They had sweet faces with an air of innocence and wide-set brown eyes. I laughed. "Do they squeak when hugged?"

Helen chuckled. "Yes, they're cute. They're miniature Cheviots. My husband and I used to show them, so they're all registered."

"Are they for sale? I bet they're expensive. Are they good for working dogs?"

"They have easygoing personalities, so, yes, they're great for working. Right now, I don't have any I can let go of. They're triple the price you're paying for the Barbs. By the time these wethers go to sale, the new crop of Cheviots will be available."

Insanely, I felt let down, like someone had taken a friend away. If the animals were available now, I couldn't have afforded them anyway.

The wind whipped up, blowing leaves and small bits of gravel into a miniature whirlwind. I pulled my hood up against the sudden chill. The debris traveled upward, and I turned to protect my eyes.

Beyond the Cheviot pen, just past a tree line, a movement caught my eye. Two coyotes scampered off as if they had been watching and fled when I noticed them. *You wily critters seem to be almost everywhere I go.*

"The Barbs are over here," Helen said to reclaim my attention, but the chill from seeing the coyotes and the fascination with the Cheviots held me in place.

As he walked off with Bita, Luke turned to me.

"Okay, I'm coming," I finally said.

The Barbados wethers were about three feet tall with slender bodies. Except for their black faces, legs, and underbellies, they looked even more like deer than the ones at the trial.

"Oh my," I said as I approached. "These guys are cute, too. Not as amazing as the Cheviots, but there're sweet."

Suddenly, something Helen had said clicked into recognition, and my stomach rolled over. "Wait, when you were talking about the sale of the wethers before… did you mean sale to the slaughterhouse when they can no longer be worked?"

Helen pursed her lips and nodded. "The nine you are buying today should be worth enough per pound that you will make a sizable profit. You'll to be able to purchase six weaned Cheviot ewes."

"But how can I look into their faces every day, then take them to the sale?" A vision crossed my mind of a brown, hairy leg on a plate.

"By honoring their choice," Helen said. Her green eyes peered at me through red-framed glasses, willing me to understand that this was something important to her.

"Their choice? Animals make choices?"

"Yes." Helen walked toward her house. Changing direction, the wind blew her salt-and-pepper hair away from her face. "Come with me," she called over her shoulder.

Luke was still staring at the sheep intently.

"Luke, here." I patted my leg.

He spun around three times, then looked at the sheep as if he couldn't believe we were leaving.

"We'll come back. I promise. Luke, here."

Reluctantly, he joined us. We walked to the house and entered through a side door.

"All these windows face east," I said. "This long room must be brilliant with the morning sun."

"Yes, it certainly is."

Bita went directly to a white stone fireplace and lay on a large, cushiony bed. The fireplace was as tall as I was and at least five feet wide. I expected to see a vase of magical Floo powder, with Harry Potter standing in the center. Instead, there were warm coals from a morning fire.

Photos of the Andes Mountains and amber-skinned, people covered one wall. The occupants were dressed in brightly colored ponchos. The men had woven caps with flaps that came over their ears, except for one, who looked like a vanilla ice cream bar in a bowl of almonds. He had blond hair, light skin, and wore white linen.

"Who's the fair-haired guy?" I asked.

"My father-in-law, Gunter. He was an archeologist who went to the Andes to study the healing practices of the Q'ero healers." Helen chuckled. "Stayed twenty years. Married the daughter of a chieftain."

"So, Mark is the golden-skinned man?" I gestured to a photo of Helen and a tall, smiling man with hair and skin almost the same rich honey color. "How did you two ever meet?"

"In college. He came to the states to get a formal education, met me and stayed. His father would laugh and say, "Leave it to a woman to lead your life in a completely different direction than you planned." My husband's family spoke three languages: English, Spanish, and Quechua. Quechua is the original native tongue of Peru, only used now by the medicine men and women."

"Look at all those crystals," I said. "Let me see, there's amber, turquoise, bloodstone, and yellow citrine. I don't know the rest. And some are carved into animals." I picked up a citrine coyote and shook my head. "These guys follow me everywhere. There's a llama, an eagle, a snake, a jaguar...oh, and a hummingbird. I love hummingbirds. Are these totems of some kind used by your husband's people?"

"Not totems. The healers observed animals and used their traits as archetypal symbols."

"Well, there's that word again. Chris used archetypal patterns to help me at the Bart Bromstead clinic."

"Uh-oh. Did he get carried away?"

"No, he helped me, actually."

"I've known Chris a long time and love him. I'm glad he helped you."

My new friend moved to a large butterscotch-colored leather sofa. "Speaking of help, have a seat. If you wish, I'll share parts of a very different belief system, beliefs that, in some ways, are opposite to us Western folk. It took a while to understand or embrace them as my own, but when I did, it helped me. I struggled with the same thoughts as you about the animals. Once you hear them, you can decide for yourself."

I nodded. "Please. My stomach gets funky every time the thought of sale or slaughter comes up, and that's been quite often lately."

"Every being," Helen began, "animals included, makes a choice before they are born into earth form as to what their purpose will be."

"Choice?" I raised an eyebrow. "You're telling me that an animal makes a choice before it's born to be eaten?" Frowning, I added, "We all have a choice?"

"That's the belief of many ancient earth traditions. To pity an animal for its offering of sustenance is to negate or dishonor its purpose. Pity dishonors its ultimate choice to be of service to the human race."

That sentence struck me. I felt the truth of it.

"Being raised in a family of carnivores," I said, "our food came packaged nicely from a market. This is the first time it's felt personal, like my friends with sweet faces are going to end up chewed up and digested by someone. I never would have dreamed a choice could be involved."

"When your diet pulls on your heartstrings, it might mean you either need to be a vegetarian or change how you view the animal," Helen said. "For me, it's how the livestock are raised that's important. So, if the animals give themselves to us to be used as food, clothing, furniture, and sometimes shelter, our job is to give back. To treat them with respect and kindness while they're alive. Many of the native cultures honor the animals with prayer and gratitude, and wish them well on the journey back to spirit. They feel the animals know their physical existence is a temporary container."

Slowly, I made sense of what Helen was saying. Rubbing my temples, I said, "I think I understand."

"I raise cattle and sheep. Every animal stays here until the time of harvest."

My eyebrows lifted. "Harvest?"

"Harvest" is the word organic and natural meat processers sometimes use instead of slaughter. It seems less violent. The livestock here never have to endure the stockyard confinement where they are overfed grain and shot with growth hormones. Every precaution is taken to see that the animals are honored and respected."

"That means my wethers can go directly to harvest." The word *harvest* still made my stomach turn over. "They will be well cared for. No problem with the grateful part either. I felt that already."

Then another thought surfaced, and I took in a breath. "How do I know I'm not just saying that so I don't feel bad?"

Helen let out a smooth laugh. "That's a question we all ask ourselves when we're changing a belief that has to do with guilt or pity. The underlying emotion you are feeling about the sheep is one of the two. Instead of feeling respect for their life choice, you are only thinking about their death."

"It's kinda hard not to think about their death when they die." But an elusive thought danced around my mind, and finally, I grabbed hold of it. "When the underlying guilt around death is not there, I have an open space in my heart for life, respect, and appreciation."

Helen's eyes danced. "The reaction we have to every relationship, whether it's happy, sad, pity, anger, or joy, is all a reflection of what we carry inside." She crossed her hands over her heart.

I raked my short hair back with both hands and rested my palms on my neck. "Wow. Animals bring all of those emotions up from time to time. Makes you look at them differently and appreciate them more. To think a being would give themselves so others can survive, or to be a show horse that someone takes their anger out on."

Then a realization touched me so deeply my throat felt tight. I gasped, "They come to us so we can learn. Luke's and my journey together makes sense. He chose me, I have no doubt. He is my teacher." I felt shaky.

Helen placed her hand over mine. "I think you got it, my dear. And I have to say, it feels wonderful to share some of my husband's ancestral wisdom. Mark was one of my greatest teachers. Because of him, I view the world differently."

The clock on the wall chimed one. "Goodness, I'd better get the sheep loaded up," I said.

Luke, knowing that five-letter word all too well, jumped up from his place by the sofa.

"Bita," Helen said. "You stay here. I'll be back soon." She scratched under the dog's chin. "I know you don't like staying when there's work to be done. But it's Luke's turn right now."

As we walked down the path to the pen, Helen said, "I won't have my girl much longer. And, boy, she's been a good one. I have two of her pups, nice dogs the both of them, but they don't hold a candle to Bita."

Words didn't feel like the right thing at the moment. I nodded and smiled in acknowledged sympathy.

We stopped just outside the pen containing the wethers. "Have you done any shedding with your dog?" Helen asked.

I shook my head. "Very little."

"There are thirty wethers in that pen. You need nine. Go in and work all thirty for a few minutes to let him run off some steam. Then, I'll help you separate them, or in herding terms—shed them."

At my command, Luke left my side and went to the sheep. He ran to the twelve o'clock position behind them beautifully and began to walk behind them horizontally.

"We've never worked more than four or five at a time. That's a whole herd," I said in excitement, with only a slight bit of trepidation. "He's not sure how to move them forward."

"What he's doing is called waring," Helen explained, watching Luke's movements with appreciation. "It will feel strange to you, but he'll have to move sideways to move them forward. See him go a little past the last sheep on each side? That dog is naturally tucking in his corners."

A sudden realization swept over me. "This is honest-to-goodness ranch work. We're official. It's *fun*."

"Now, call him to you. Once he's there, tell him to stay. Then walk away. Call him when you've started a path through the sheep. Then move in and help him shed off the ones toward the gate."

I did as Helen instructed. Luke hesitated and looked side to side, a little confused about coming through the middle. But finally at my insistence, he walked along the path I had made down the middle of the herd. Helen had opened the gate. Then she quickly ran in to hold the remaining sheep back while Luke and I walked the nine into the alleyway. Soon, the three of us were driving the sheep straight toward the open doors of my trailer. Luke tucked in his corners as all nine animals vaulted inside.

"Luke, here," I shouted. He exited the trailer, and Helen and I shut the two large doors.

Helen brushed her hands together. "That went great."

It had. Accomplishing the everyday farm chore felt as if Luke and I had done something monumental. It might have been an afterglow from the talk Helen and I just had, or it might have simply been admiration of my dog—the handsome boy I had thought might never have an interest in working. Whatever the cause, I thought I might explode with joy and pride.

While handing a check to Helen for our nine new sheep, I said, "Thank you for all the help today. I loved learning about the healing cultures. And I do feel better."

"Glad to do it. It helps me to stay centered when I work with others. So you did the both of us some good."

"There's something else..." I frowned slightly. "Thanks for not bringing up that judge guy, Bart."

"It's really not my business. You put him in his place, and he needed it. He's got something stuck in his craw, but only he can work it out. Now, you and your dog enjoy those boys." She pointed to the trailer. "I'm working with two young dogs and would love some company, so come back anytime. Be safe going home."

Two hours later, we pulled onto our drive past the sign that said, "Dream Maker Ranch: Horse Training, Sales, and Instruction." I smiled and thought, *One day, I might have to add "Sheep Farming."*

Chapter Twenty

After hearing me pull into the drive, Sharon leaned the pooper-scooper against a stall wall and came to help. The fuchsia-pink stripe in her dark, curly hair bounced wildly as she ran and opened the pasture gate.

My mind was preoccupied with the experience at Helen's when I should have been thinking about the best way to introduce what amounted to young orphaned children to a new environment.

Luke and Sharon stood with me as I opened the trailer door. All nine wethers firmly pressed against the front panel, like brown furry sardines.

"Away to me," I said.

Luke jumped into the right side of the trailer, ran down the wall, and peeled the babies off the panel.

The deer-like creatures came bounding out at a dead run with Luke right behind them.

After a long blast from my whistle, Luke's belly hit the ground. The next few minutes seemed like weeks as my mind processed what was happening. These babies didn't react like any of the other sheep we had worked. They didn't slow down or stop when my dog took the pressure off by lying down.

Nine terrified creatures ran to the only place they sensed to be security: the three brood mares that were grazing at the highest point of the hay meadow. By the time I realized where they were headed, it was too late to send Luke.

"Why are they running to the horses?" shouted Sharon.

Realization inched into my mind as I stood transfixed. "We just weaned their foals, so the mares smell of milk. They have four legs, warm bodies, and don't make clanging noises."

The horror of what happened next would haunt me for a very long time.

The broodmares wanted no part in providing shelter or security for the new orphans. The babies were pushing and shoving each other, which did nothing but strike the mares' engorged udders with their tiny horns. All three horses bucked and kicked with abandon. One wether flew six feet into the air. After rolling over and over across the ground, he rose and ran for the fence. With one giant leap, the animal disappeared into the neighbor's pasture. The next sheep to be kicked into flight landed in a heap and stayed there.

Sharon, Luke, and I took off running toward a chaos of high-pitched screeches from the mares and bawling bleats from the wethers. Hooves and sheep were flying everywhere.

A black blur caught my attention. It was Luke, running to the twelve o'clock position behind the tragedy happening before me. He crouched low, moving forward and looking for a place to intervene. My dog had not one ounce of fear of the horses, but he did have a burning instinct to get the sheep to me, even if it meant getting hurt.

"Luke, get back." My panicked shout was so loud, my throat felt like sandpaper. He turned immediately and trotted back ten yards.

"Luke, down, stay," I croaked. Then I said a brief internal thank-you to Colby, who had spent the last training session with us teaching Luke the look-back and get-back commands. I had witnessed a dog killed instantly by a horse. The well-intending animal had intervened when a horse had refused to enter a trailer. The unexpected kick had sent the dog flying, never to rise again. My hands felt as if they had been pricked with a million needles. His obedience to commands might have just saved his life.

"We're not going to be able to get the sheep away from the horses," I shouted. "We have to get the horses away from the sheep." I looked at the woman a few yards away. "Wave your hands and shout, Sharon! Run, go, go, go!"

In an instant, we were waving our hands wildly and running straight for the horses. "Scram, you guys, get out of here," I belted.

The girls were all too happy to take one last jump and gallop to the other end of the pasture.

One sheep stood alone, his lower lip dangling so far off its face that it resembled a bright red bib. A pool of blood formed at his feet. Another, huddled with the others, had a gash on his shoulder. Of the nine Barbados, one had disappeared completely, and three were injured to some degree. The remaining five stood huddled and shaking, too frightened to bleat.

"What a mess," Sharon whispered.

"Go call Eastside Vet Clinic," I ordered. "Get Dr. Ward or Seidenberger out. Quickly, please." Panting, I ran to the sheep on the ground who, amazingly, was still alive.

Sharon's voice was shrill. "For a twenty dollar sheep?"

"Please," I insisted.

"Okay." Sharon lifted her chin and placed a defiant hand on her hip. "It's after five o'clock, so you will not only pay for a farm call but an after-hours emergency call."

"Sharon, go."

The unhappy woman took off at a trot for the barn.

With a strangely calm detachment, I walked over to Luke and said, "Walk up."

He slowly rose to a crouch. With his nose about six inches off the ground, he urged the exhausted babies to a walk. We made a quiet procession down the hay meadow and into the pen.

After I closed the gate, I found myself sitting on the ground in the hay meadow with the injured sheep's upper body in my lap. Immersed in guilt, I had no recollection of how I had gotten there.

His eyes stared blankly, his chest barely moving with shallow breaths.

My calm detachment shattered in a memory of echoed pain. It felt as if looking at the wounded animal in my lap had been the start button of an old video. I could see my father clearly as he loomed over my five-year-old self and pointed at my chest. "It's your fault your grandmother lost her rooster."

And he had been right. It had been my fault. I had been thoughtless when I ran into my grandmother's chicken yard, and I had been thoughtless today. The first act had resulted in a trip to the army hospital and painful stitches in my head. Today's thoughtlessness resulted in harm coming to four innocent babies.

Helen had entrusted me with the very animals she treated with gratitude and respect. I had assumed responsibility and now... now, at least four had grievous injuries. I had no idea how badly the one that jumped the fence in a panic had faired.

"I'm so sorry," I said, and began to sob uncontrollable, gasping sobs.

After some time, I became aware of the ground underneath me and Luke lying beside me. The sobs ebbed away and the stains on my heart dulled. I reached in my pocket, pulled out a tattered tissue, and wiped the river of snot streaming from my nose. I blotted the tears with my sleeve, took in a deep breath, and thought of my conversation with Helen. I felt a connection slowly forming deep down beneath the numbness.

The evening pinks, reds, oranges, and blues reminded me of an Indian sunset. A Lakota prayer came to mind. *The Earth is my Mother, she holds me so sweetly; The Sun, Moon, and Stars are my Father, he comforts and warms me.*

Sitting on my hilltop sanctuary, I felt the connection of sky and earth so deeply I shuddered. That's when I knew this sweet, barely breathing baby in my lap had a purpose.

"Did you really make a choice to be here on this earth with all its wonder and beauty, with all its tragedy and horror? If you have a spiritual choice"—I stroked the sweet black face—"we all must have a choice. So many animals are abused and neglected every day either out of suppressed human anger, ignorance or, like me, thoughtlessness."

I swiped at the tears under my chin. "Each time an animal comes into a tragic situation, the human has an opportunity to make a different choice, choices they are often unaware of, and precious animals allow us the choice." The wonder of the realization held me enthralled, and the gratitude I felt could not be expressed.

Suddenly, Luke rose in a ferocious bark. Startled, I turned to see Dr. Lincoln Ward approaching us.

"Hey, buddy," Dr. Ward said. "You know me." The veterinarian stood still until Luke circled him once and sat at his feet. Then the dark-haired man roughed my still-timid dog a big rough around the collar.

"Sharon said you had injured sheep," he said in his usual professional manner. "I saw the three in the pen. Fixable enough."

"Three?"

"Yes, laceration on shoulder, lip hanging, and one with a swelling hip. Let's see what's up with this one." His businesslike demeanor softened as we looked at each other. "Naomi, are you all right?"

I gave him a weak smile. "Yes, I'm okay. Had a little meltdown is all."

"Scared me for a minute," the vet said. "In all my years of coming out here, I've never seen you quite so emotionally charged. Can you get up so I can take a look?" He held his hand out to help me. His smile brought warmth to his prom-king good looks.

"Oh yeah, I guess I'd better." I took his hand and got to my feet.

After examining the animal, the vet said. "He's been kicked in the abdomen. No blood on his mouth, so if he's bleeding internally, it's slow. No broken bones that I can tell. Without surgery, I can only put him on fluids and monitor him. I'll have to take him to the clinic."

I nodded.

Soon, I was an emergency room assistant to a veterinarian suturing sheep. When that job was done, Dr. Ward transported the wether to Eastside Veterinary Clinic. Sadly, Dr. Ward phoned three hours later to say that the sheep had passed. The baby's internal injuries had been too severe to save him.

Chapter Twenty-One

"This long, boring ride to the Oklahoma Panhandle sure is better with company," Colby said. "Sharing fuel expense doesn't hurt either." She glanced toward the back of my truck, where her two dogs were crated. "I'm sure they're happy to be getting to trial again."

"Glad to have the company," I replied. "Luke's a good road guy, but not the greatest conversationalist."

"You've learned a lot in the last few months. I think you two are ready for a larger trial."

"I hope so." I thought about him grabbing the sheep's leg and the mouth full of fur he finished the run with. "No more hair-pulling sheep-wrecks." I laughed.

The road we took to the trial grounds wound us along the Cimarron River. Due to recent rain, the waterway flowed swiftly toward Kansas. Pillar-like ponderosa pines, oak trees, and golden currant bushes bordered the trial grounds. The huge acreage smelled of freshly mowed prairie grass and a slight scent of ozone.

The sun insisted on making an appearance. It cast a blue-and-gold halo of light around the dark clouds. We drove past white tent awnings that served as covers for the sign-in table, judge's stand, and viewing gallery. We parked at the opposite end near a rather small fenced arena where the novice classes would be held.

"The wind's cold," Colby said as she buttoned her coat. "It's going to rain, for sure."

Shivering, I wrapped my arms around myself. "I'm glad I brought umbrellas."

As we approached the spot where the running order was posted, I noticed a familiar small woman with curly salt-and-pepper hair.

"Hi," Helen exclaimed and hugged me. She pointed to the board with the lists. "I see you're in the novice. So am I, with my two young dogs. Colby, you're in classes five and eight of the ranch division. Bart has one in the pro-novice and one in the ranch."

Hearing his name brought the black-hatted cad of a judge to the forefront of my mind. My insides quivered with electric apprehension. Hiding my unease with a chuckle, I said, "Well, I knew I would run into him sometime."

Noticing the small size and low fences of the novice arena, I grew more uneasy. Then the wind brought up the stench of sheep urine, rotted leaves, and manure. The repulsive smell added nausea to my nervous twitters. "Helen, I don't like the looks of that arena. It's small."

"I thought about that," Helen said. "For my young dogs, it's fine. They're slower and quieter when they work. I've noticed how much more comfortable Luke is in big fields. The dog is so fast he has room to run, room to bring the sheep back into line if they get off track. I agree, that arena might be trouble."

"So, what can I do about it?"

"Well, you can advance him to the pro-novice. It's held in the big field by the river. He would have plenty of space to bring the sheep into alignment if they wandered. Instead of just bringing them down the field and penning them, he would have to maneuver them around you, then drive them away and guide them around a freestanding fence panel. After the panel, he would bring them back to you and put them in the pen."

My eyes grew round at the thought of the river. I had learned, however, that sheep could swim.

"I see Luke move the sheep away from you and around the cedar trees all the time," Colby said.

"What little I've seen him drive he does okay," Helen said. "In fact, herding dogs are instinctively gathering dogs, and typically have difficulty taking sheep away from a handler. Luke doesn't seem to have any problem with it."

I blew out a breath. "I don't know."

"There's one other thing you need to consider," Helen added. "If you show him in the pro-novice today, he can never go back to the novice. If you have a problem, Luke is in that level, or above, for the rest of his career."

Ropes of indecision tugged me in all directions. I couldn't let Luke have another bad experience—not because of embarrassment but because we were creating habits. I didn't want bad habits I might not be able to break. In the small arena, we would be in a relatively controlled environment, but that environment would not suit his working style. The large field held no safe fences. Although I had more control and understanding of the task, I knew all too well what a sheep magnet the perimeter could be.

I paced back and forth. There was also the chance of thunder to consider. I wasn't sure how to factor a booming sky into the event.

"What do I have to do if I want to move up?" I asked Colby.

"Tell the show secretary so she can change the running orders before the trial starts. She will take you off the novice list and add you to the bottom of the pro-novice." Helen glanced at her watch. "You have ten minutes."

Finally, I said, "Well, bull hockey." The instant I decided, the turmoil in my belly eased, only to be replaced by a sense of urgency. I took off running for the sign-in table, yelling to my friend, "Meet me at the truck, Colby. Luke and I are moving up a class."

The day grew darker, and a fine misty rain cast a fog-like veil around us. The small arena soon became a mire. By the time they left the arena, dogs and sheep were covered in smelly mud.

As I watched Helen work her first dog, I noticed a similarity to

Colby. Both women worked softly and calmly at all times, even when things went wrong. Both women read the subtle body language of the sheep and instructed their dogs before the sheep veered in the wrong direction or stopped altogether. So that's why they often had less difficulty than some of the other handlers. They sensed trouble before it happened and avoided most mishaps. Ah, to be an experienced shepherdess. Could that ever be me?

"What a mess," Helen said as she walked out the gate. She ran her slender fingers through wet curls that clung to her face. "Too bad their first outing has to be under these conditions." Helen knelt and roughed her dog's neck. "What a good boy, Flick. Let's get you a drink." As she rose, she said, "You're last to run in your class, so you can watch a few of the pro-novice dogs. Grab us some chairs under the awning. I'll be right there."

The first two dogs in the category completed their runs without a hitch, but the third one ran in too close. Soon, all four sheep were bolting through the trees, jumping bushes, and heading straight for the river. The dog's handler whistled one command after another, but the dog wouldn't respond. I couldn't tell if the animal couldn't hear over the wind or was blatantly ignoring his handler, but both options filled me with fear. What if Luke made the same mistake?

I felt giant hands squeezing my chest. Once I recognized my self-sabotage, I took charge. *No, no, no,* I told my wayward brain. *See it play out like you want it to happen.* I took a deep breath and saw a mental image of Luke executing a perfect outrun, lift, fetch, drive, and pen.

After that lovely scene had a firm hold in my head, I breathed normally again.

A dark-headed female judge blew a whistle, and my breath caught in my throat. I felt pity for the man at the handler's post.

"Call your dog in, please." She glanced at a man to her right and nodded.

The male competitor gave an unbelievably loud, shrill blast from his whistle. Within seconds, his small black-and-white dog came running out of the woods toward him.

The man on her right rose and walked over to a red Border Collie lying under the awning. "Chloe, go-by."

The dog took off though the trial field and headed for the woods.

In less than five minutes, four crazed animals covered with wet leaves and mud erupted from the woods, followed by the red dog.

Just as the sheep cleared the tree line, the sandy-haired man whistled a bobwhite sound.

The dog turned all four St. Croix to her right toward the holding pen at the far end of the field, where another man opened the gate.

Once the sheep were secured, Chloe ran back down the field to her handler.

"I'm always impressed with Dan's dogs," said Colby.

"Wow, just wow," I said. "She listened, worked independently, and turned the sheep away from him at a distance. I hope Luke and I can work like that when we grow up."

Helen glanced at the man praising his dog. "That's Dan Pickle, one of the best around. He's won the USBCHA Nationals three times."

The three of us sat in silence and watched the next dog work.

"Naomi..." Helen hesitated as if she was thinking as she spoke. "If you ever want someone to do some extensive training with Luke, Dan would be a good choice. He's a positive, firm trainer who takes good care of his dogs. You, of all people, would understand the importance of having someone experienced work with your boy."

I mulled her suggestion around in my mind. Logically, I knew she was right. My heart and brain, however, were at odds. Finally, my heart won, and I said, "Luke lived alone in a kennel the first nine months of his life. I promised him he would never endure a storm alone in a kennel again. If he went for training, he would be housed outside, and I won't do that to him. He sleeps by my bed and that's it."

"I understand." Helen's smile held a river of sadness. "Bita slept by my bed for fourteen years and still kept a good work ethic. But when I tried it with my young boys, they quit listening. I had to take them back to the kennels, and they seem happier there."

"Four more dogs, then me," I said shortly. I knew that Helen meant well, but I would sooner sleep in a kennel myself than shatter my dog's sense of security and trust.

A light, steady rain set in as we approached the handler's post. With an umbrella in one hand, my crook in the other, and my whistle hanging at my chest, I was ready. Luke didn't notice the rain or the distant thunder. All he saw were the four white specks at the far end of the field. After three spins, he settled enough for me to send him.

"Go-by," was the only verbal command I used through the entire run. After hours of practicing with my whistle, no spit drooled down my chin. Only clear, precise tones directed my dog around the course.

As if we had shared the same mind when I visualized our run, we had an almost flawless class. We had two minor deductions that I knew of: when he lifted the sheep from the back too quickly and when two wooly animals veered off during the drive.

Luke had them back straight in no time. Despite the cold, despite the rain, despite my sopping wet dog, standing at the pen gate and seeing all four sheep run inside left me giddy. Between the rain and my tear-swimming eyes, I could barely see to direct Luke and the sheep back to the holding pen. I waited until we had exited the field to drop to my knees and hug him.

After Colby competed with her dogs, we returned to my truck. I let the diesel engine run just long enough to defog the windshield and warm us up.

"Bart had a dog in my class," I said. "How'd he do?"

"He had a good run, but he stayed close to the arena while you ran, and watched every move you and Luke made. The sour expression on his face sure didn't belong on the Bart I know."

"Okay, it's time to get to the bottom of what's going on with him. This has gotten old. It's sad to think I worked so hard to get here, and someone dislikes me. I'll talk to him at the end of the day and make amends."

A tap on my window drew my attention.

Helen smiled broadly and pointed toward the largest awning.

My heartbeat fluttered. "The placings must be posted for

our classes." Glancing in the backseat, I said, "We'll be right back, handsome."

Ears still wet, eyes bright, tongue lolling, Luke sat up and looked out the window.

My hand shook slightly as I opened the truck door. Could we have placed? Could Luke's and my name really be one of the five names on the pro-novice results sheet? How could we be? We had two deductions that I knew of. Who knew what other mistakes we made?

Colby, Helen, and I huddled with several other people under the awning. The only empty space was right in front of Bart. The simple act of standing near the man added to my tremors. I stepped on my tiptoes to see the sheet beyond the person in front of me. In the span of a heartbeat, I wanted to jump into the air. I wanted to shout. I wanted to hug everyone around.

Instead, I gave my best impression of nonchalance, as though placing at a trial happened all the time. Luke's and my names were posted on the sheet. Rodger White handed me an envelope with 2nd Place written on the front. He smiled, winked, and mouthed, "You go, girl."

Colby and Helen both received checks from placing in their classes.

"Do you think you deserved that prize?" The heat from Bart's baritone whisper behind me felt as if a family of spiders had crawled down my spine. "Your beginner's luck is going to run out. If you were smarter, you'd sell that dog to someone who could make him what he deserves to be."

Sputtering, I spun and looked up into hard, hate-filled, dark eyes. Anger boiled inside me. When the group exited the announcer's area, I took off after Bart.

As I stomped toward his truck, I realized I hadn't lost my temper. I knew exactly where it was. It exploded in a rush. "What's wrong with you?" I spat out. "What did I ever do to you?"

"Oh, I think you know," he sneered coldly.

"No, I don't. You're cruel and spiteful for no other reason than because you can be. Why don't you just leave me and my dog alone?"

I elbowed past him and walked away as calmly as my shaking body would allow, not stopping until my feet reached my truck.

"So much for making friends with the man," I responded to Colby's raised brows. "Looks like that's never going to happen."

"Helen said to tell you goodbye and that she'll see you next week. She had to get home. I got everything loaded while you were gone. Let's hit the road."

Once we were in the truck with the motor running, I said, "Let's see what you won, Mr. Luke."

The damp envelope contained eighty dollars. Our first time to compete in an open field, and we had actually earned prize money. "Wow, Colby, my entry fee was thirty, so we netted fifty. Pretty great." I said the words, but I didn't feel them.

We deserved excitement and celebration. Instead, I felt only a hollow dread.

Chapter Twenty-Two

During the night, our mid-March rain had turned into an ice-and-snow storm. White-mantled cedar trees reminded me of miniature mountains. My feet crunched on frozen bluestem grass as Luke and I walked west, eighty yards away from seven Barbados wethers. Little wisps of fog formed when my breath hit the chilly air.

We turned to face the east just as the sun peeked over the Miller farm. The giant golden orb turned the sky a crystal blue. I took in a slow breath and savored the sparkling fairy-tale image before me.

The next thing I saw left me giggling. Then the giggles erupted into a laugh, which became a belly roll.

All seven of the fully-grown creatures in their fuzzy winter wool bounded toward us in complete joyous abandon. They were leaping straight up into the air, turning, and twisting in half so far that their tails almost reached their noses. The black-and-tan boys had been worked so much they knew Luke would be coming for them. *Here we go*, they must have thought.

Before I could regain my composure, Luke and I were circled by the leaping creatures as if we were standing in the center of a carousel. My dog looked up at me, tilted his head, and seemed to ask, *What now?* We just stood there while the sheep continued their joyful play. I wiped a gloved hand at the happy tears streaming down my face.

"Get out," I said through a bubble of laughter. Luke ran to the west twenty yards.

My stomach gave a little twitter at his instant response to my command. "Walk up."

Luke slowly padded forward, driving the bouncing boys away from me and toward the cedar trees.

The utter happiness of the sheep had been infectious. But as I watched Luke creep along behind the boys in the crouched posture of an honest-to-goodness talented Border Collie, my heart skipped. *This. This feeling.* This was better, stronger, purer, than any time Luke and I had spent in competition. At peace in this crystalline wonderland, I realized what true happiness felt like—me and my dog and the sheep swirling around us.

The animals romping before me lived in the now. They didn't regret the past. They didn't worry about the future. They were at a place of joyful peace. Their demonstration of that joy filled me with awe. Suddenly, I knew that how I lived each moment created another one just like it. Every atom and molecule in my body tingled with the truth of it.

The metal whistle tasted cold. I softly blew the sound of a bobwhite, and Luke made a slight clockwise turn. The sheep wound through the trees.

My mind continued to wander. *I'm human. Crappy things and crappy people happen. Butthead judges can show up to cause tension and doubt when we should be celebrating.*

How do I hold on to the joy in these moments? How in the world can I get that man's comments out of my head?

As the sheep came around a tree, all seven Barbados took off for the pond, still bounding and jumping.

That brought on another laugh. Life always seemed to have unexpected turns.

I gave a wolf whistle. Luke zipped around counterclockwise and headed them back to me.

Too bad I couldn't whistle the man away, or at least understand why he had so much animosity toward me.

In that moment of absolute peace, clarity, and joy, I purposefully created a memory. Then I closed my eyes and bound it in my heart. I could call upon the memory when life had runaway turns that brought hurt and shadows. I could think of these moments as a happy-charm or a joy-spell that could displace the dark. No one could take them away. No one could dispel the happiness I felt on this glorious day in the hay meadow with Luke, my partner.

"Let's go in," I told Luke.

As we made our way to the barn, I knew I had to face something I would rather not. It was time for my boy to have new animals to work. I took in a breath, assessing my sheep situation. Colby had graciously let me breed two of my original sheep, Sally and Sue, to her Cheviot ram. With them back home now, we were happily anticipating the first sheep births at Dream Maker Ranch. However, that didn't solve my immediate working dilemma.

"Another week and the Cheviot ewes will be ready to wean," Helen had said during a phone conversation. "Bring your Barbados to me. I'll take care of transporting them to the sale. In the meantime, Colby has some St. Croix she's working. Give her a call."

"Yes!" Colby said, a few hours later. "Come tomorrow if you can. I'm starving for someone to talk to besides my dogs and a toddler."

"We'll be there around ten in the morning."

On the way the next day, Luke paced the backseat of my truck. "Yeah, you know we're going somewhere to work, don't you? This time it's Colby's." I checked the rearview mirror. "Uh-oh, your crate's sliding around. I forgot to bungee it down." I pulled over to the side of the road.

Jumping down from the driver's seat, I leapt into the back. While I secured Luke's crate, the reverberating blast of a truck's airhorn blew panic through me. I jerked upright and looked around.

Half sitting, half standing, head turning, eyes darting—Luke was in the middle of the northbound lane of Highway 412. A John Deere green tanker truck bore down on him at full speed.

All eighteen tires locked up. The asphalt screeched. I smelled burning rubber.

Like in a slow-motion replay, the tank started moving sideways into a jackknife.

"Oh, sh—." I vaulted from the side of my truck and opened the rear door as my feet hit the pavement. In two giant leaps, I scooped up Luke like he was a powderpuff.

I threw him across the backseat and slammed the door milliseconds before the truck slid by us. Smoke billowing from the tires left an acrid taste in my throat.

As soon as the truck passed, and the horror of what could have happened to my dog hit my brain, I began to shake uncontrollably. I rested my forehead against the rear-door window of my truck. I gasped for air.

The driver pulled the tanker onto the shoulder far in front of me. He jumped out of his cab and ran toward me. He shouted, "You all right, ma'am?"

Unable to speak, I nodded and lifted a finger.

He looked around and asked, "Where's the dog?"

I pointed to the backseat.

"Hope he's okay. Thought for sure he was a goner."

The man was short, round, and balding, his eyes filled with concern. His dark green uniform looked like it had just been pressed. His name, John, was embroidered above his left shirt pocket.

"There's a bottle of water in my truck," he said. "Can I get it for you?"

"No thanks," I gasped. "Might be sick."

After I caught my breath, I said, "I forgot to bungee his crate down. When I noticed it moving around, I pulled over to the shoulder and got out to fasten it."

"Was he lost? Spinnin' in the middle of the highway, lookin' around like that?" John asked.

"No, searching for sheep," I replied.

"In the middle of a highway?"

I held my forehead in my hands. "I'm on my way to a friend's in Blackwell to work sheep. I left the driver door partway open—he must have thought we were there and squeezed out behind it without me knowing it."

"You gonna be okay?" he asked. "Want me to call someone?"

"No. I'm fine." I flashed him a weak smile. "Thanks. Is everything all right with your truck?"

John stood up a little taller, straightened his shoulders, and said, "Yeah, I got her lined out."

As I watched the man walk away, I remembered Luke.

I opened the truck door to find Luke shaking, huddled in the corner. He turned his head and cowered when I reached in to touch him, something he hadn't done since the first day I got him. Not to *me*.

"Sweetheart, I'm so, so sorry."

My entire body went weak. I crawled in, sat beside him, and laid my hand on his back for several minutes. When he didn't respond, I decided not to push him. But I did run my hands all over his body to check for broken bones. Relieved that at least nothing was physically broken, I called Colby, left a message that we weren't coming and turned around to go home.

Charlie, the man from whom I had purchased Luke, had semi-neglected him because of his wife's illness, but I was sure Luke had never been physically harmed... until now. No, it was me who'd let him come into harm's way and then thrown him like a rag doll across the seat and brutally banged him into a door.

During the two-hour drive back home, the lack of Luke's eager pacing, along with not seeing his expectant eyes reflected in the rearview mirror, tore my heart into tiny pieces. What if I had lost what I had tried so long to create? What if I had just let a rush of fear and adrenaline shatter his trust in me?

When we arrived, Sharon's car stood in the parking lot, two hours after her normal time to leave.

When I tried to put my arms around my dog to lift him out of the seat, he backed away. To my great relief, he did let me fasten his leash.

When I tugged slightly, he jumped right out. I knelt and held his face in my hands. "Are you okay?" His response was to look away.

I unfastened the leash, and he trotted off into the barn.

Grinning, Sharon greeted me at the door. "Come and see them. They're the cutest things ever to walk the earth."

"Sharon, I'm not in the mood."

"You are for this." The woman grabbed my arm and pulled me in the direction Luke had gone.

"Sharon, really. Don't." I stepped away.

"Luke's going to see them before you do if you don't come on." She did a little bouncing jig down the barn aisle.

Giving in, I followed her.

Mac's face held a reverent but excited expression as he toweled a tiny, doll-like infant lamb. An infant so precious that, despite my fear and anxiety over Luke, I smiled.

"You just missed the excitement," he said.

The tiny white lamb had the short, perky ears, wide-set eyes and the spindly legs of the Cheviots I had fallen in love with.

"I delivered them. Me." Sharon pointed to her chest with her thumb.

"Them?" I glanced around to find two more identical babies suckling from Sally's udders. "Three?"

"Yes, triplets," Sharon said. "I noticed Sally at the back gate right after you left. She was panting like she'd been runnin' for miles. I brought her into the pen with the fresh straw you made ready for delivery time."

I looked over at Mac.

"I didn't come in until it was all over." He shrugged. "Midwife Sharon did it all."

"Sally made the most terrible squealing sound and fell to the ground, then got up and paced, but nothing happened. When she fell again, I thought she might die." Sharon stood up straighter and puffed out her chest. "I decided to make the call to Eastside Vet Clinic. All the vets were busy, but Doctor Ward talked me through what to do. One baby was in a butt-first position. It was scary, I have to tell ya. I had the phone at my ear and my arm up Sally's... well, you know."

"Good job, Sharon," I said. "But wait... you called Eastside? On your own?" My brows went up.

"Well..." My helper cast her eyes in the sheep's direction, her face flushed with wonder. "These ladies are special, and I couldn't let a girl die in pain no matter how much she was worth. I guess all these hairy creatures around here have grown on me. Besides, I knew what you would do."

"Thank you." I hugged her. "You saved the day."

And I ruined the day, I thought. "It's late," I told her. "You'd better get home to your kids."

During the exchange with Sharon, a part of my attention never strayed from my dog—who didn't show any signs of discomfort as he paced the perimeter of the temporary maternity ward.

"Hot chocolate sounds good right about now," Mac said. "I'll go in and make some and get these dirty clothes changed."

I nodded and sat on a hay bale to watch the new family. Luke came over and lay down by my feet, just out of reach.

"Here you go." Mac sat down beside me. "It's that really dark stuff you like."

"Thanks. I thought Sally had a few more days to go before delivery or I wouldn't have left, but it turned out okay."

"When I talked to Doctor Ward, he wanted to know how old Sally is. He said she's too old to be a candidate for breeding. Too many lambs have left her birthing muscles nonfunctioning. If Sharon hadn't acted as she did, we could have a dead sheep instead of a family of four. I guess it's common in older ewes. That's probably why Mandy sold them to you so cheap."

It felt as if a little trickle of cold water slid down my spine as a disturbing thought joined the many others rolling around unbridled in my head. I had sent my two ewes for breeding without checking to see if they were physically capable. "I'm sure Sue is in the same danger," I said.

"Your sheep investments haven't exactly paid off." Mac looked up toward the cobwebs in the rafters. "We still haven't retrieved the Barbados that ran off. One is dead, and the other eats funny. And the vet bill was outrageous. You owe me big-time for that. And it's not over yet. Sue hasn't had her baby or babies. And—"

"Stop, just stop it!" I screeched and threw the cup of chocolate down. "Why do you always make everything about money?"

Mac's eyes got very wide, and his brows rose to his hairline.

I jumped up from my chair, words exploding out in an irrational tumble. "You always bring up what I do wrong. Can't you ever tell me what I do right?"

Some little obscure part of my mind knew that Mac hadn't meant anything by his comments, but I couldn't seem to access it. Luke stood up on the bale of hay. Bootsie Myrtle watched as if amused from her perch.

Mac vaulted from his chair. "That's enough!" he shouted, lifting his hands in a stopping gesture. "You haven't thought anything through when it comes to sheep or that dog." He glanced at Luke, who jumped down from the hay behind Mac and whined—a piercing, tormented sound. Then he spun around as if he didn't know what to do.

Mac raised his voice. "Quit!"

With startling speed, Luke had rammed his nose between Mac's legs and grabbed hold of the seat of his sweatpants and undershorts. My husband jumped straight up into the air at the same time Luke pulled down. I could almost hear Luke say, "Oh no, buddy, you're not jumping away."

I stopped in mid-retort and choked out something that could have been a sob or laughter. The look of shocked horror on Mac's face was too much. My hands flew to my mouth. I tried to hold it back, but couldn't. Laughter erupted in convulsive spasms.

Mac held one hand in front, shielding his man parts from sudden exposure. With the other hand, he tried to dislodge the dog that wasn't about to let go.

"Luke," I choked out, gasping though my laughter. "That'll do."

My dog let go of Mac's britches and ran to me, still whining and clearly distraught. Luke adored Mac but wasn't about to allow him to harm me or flee the scene. After almost two years, I still hadn't heard Luke growl, but he'd taken charge of the situation the best way he knew how.

"It's okay, sweetheart." I bent down to hug my dog, relief flooding through me when he allowed it. "Dad would never hurt me."

Mac's cheeks blazed red with anger. Then he faced me. "You think this is funny?" he spat as he rearranged his clothes.

All I could do for a second was nod. Then I stood up and said, "I'm sorry. My emotions felt like a rollercoaster, and I couldn't get off. I guess what you said hit a raw spot, and I just exploded."

"Well, Luke got our attention," Mac said. A soft smile emerged, and he chuckled, an inviting sound. "He makes a good referee."

I lay my head on Mac's chest. "I really am sorry." Then I looked up into his blue eyes, "Sit down. I need to tell you about almost letting my dog get killed."

After I had told my story, he said, "Yeah, you should have closed the driver's door when you got out, but you won't make that mistake again. You reacted quickly, and that's all that matters." His eyes widened and he placed his hand on top of mine. "Did you stop to think *you* could have been killed running onto the highway like that?" Then he ran his hand over Luke's head. "You okay, buddy? Did your mom go all Incredible Hulk and Arnold Schwarzenegger on you?" Luke licked his hand. "I think we're forgiven." He looked up at me. "I think this guy and I will love you no matter what."

I sighed. It wasn't *their* love I questioned. A sudden tightness in my chest came with the realization that I seemed to always let down the ones *I* loved the most.

Chapter Twenty-Three

I 've heard a certain sound only twice in my life—a sound so piercing, so anguished, that it chilled me to the core. The first time was when my daughter fell off the back of a flatbed truck and broke her arm. The second happened one hot August evening, shortly after dark.

We had expanded the sheep pen to accommodate our growing population of miniature Cheviots. I had walked out of the barn with two full water buckets when I heard a brief, visceral scream that sent prickles of terror through me. I sat the buckets down, my senses alert and tense.

"Please, I can't tell where you are. Make another sound," I whispered.

Cloud cover made the night eerily dark. My mind whirled. It could have been a coyote, a neighbor's child, or a dog. *Dog... Where's Luke?*

Only a few moments before, I had unhooked him from his tether spot in the barn. "The sheep, you've gone to the sheep." I ducked through the fence cables and sprinted to the pen. "Luke, where are you?"

Twelve white Cheviots were luminous shadows behind the fence, but no Luke.

Just outside the sheep enclosure, I tripped over a black form and face-planted into the grass. I turned over and bolted upright, relief flooding through me as I realized that the shadow belonged to Luke. The white blaze on his face and chest were visible in the dark. "Oh, sweetheart, you're okay, it wasn't you." I stood and brushed off my jeans. "I'll water the sheep and we'll go in. Stay."

After I emptied the buckets into the water tub and closed the sheep's gate, I said, "Come on, handsome, let's go get some dinner."

The two of us walked through the pasture gate and into the barn. A whimper caught my attention, and I glanced down.

"Oh, sweet boy!" I gasped, horrified. In the dark, I hadn't noticed Luke walking on three legs. He hadn't made a single sound of distress. Luke's paw hung limply from the front leg that he held out from his body. An inch-long piece of bone protruded from a tear in his fur.

The gravity of what appeared before me penetrated my brain, and I gasped, "How did you—? How did I not notice? Shit. *Sharon*," I shouted. "Go get Mac, hurry!"

Instead of running to the house, the woman ran to me. The moment she saw me holding Luke's paw in place, she spun in the opposite direction and sprinted off.

"Grab a *Quarter Horse Journal* from the house and tell Mac to back the truck down here."

"Yes, ma'am," my helper shouted over her shoulder.

Within a few moments, I heard the diesel engine outside the back door.

"This was on the counter," Sharon said, waving the magazine, a puzzled look on her face as she ran toward me.

"Stop in the tack room and get the duct tape," I yelled.

As soon as Mac and I had stabilized Luke's fracture with the tape and magazine, we carried him to the truck and were on our way. Within a few minutes, we parked outside the Small Animal Hospital. Dr. Brian arrived shortly after.

"I'm so glad you were on call and could meet us here," I sighed.

The veterinarian patted my shoulder and knelt over Luke. "Let's get that leg X-rayed."

After a short gurney ride into the clinic and an injection of pain meds, Luke rested comfortably while Dr. Brian processed the radiographs.

"What a good boy you are," I crooned and stroked Luke's head.

"How did this happen?" asked Mac.

"I'm not sure." I scrubbed my forehead as if the motion would help me think. The sheep pen occupied one corner of a small pasture that housed two of our personal horses, Sadie and Wynonna Belle. Could they have been involved?

"I unhooked Luke so he could go with me to water the sheep." The memory of the event fell into place as I spoke. "While the buckets were filling, I heard the mares running in the pasture. For a moment, I wondered if the coyote had been stalking the new sheep. I know that creature can't get in the pen, so I wasn't worried about it."

"I'm asking you how Luke broke his leg," Mac said in irritation. "I don't need a blow-by-blow of your evening."

One, two, three, four, I thought. *Breathe.* I narrowed my eyes at my husband and said, "My brain has to work at its own pace. I know you're stressed too, but chill out, buddy. He—" I glanced at my dog. "—must have heard the commotion and run to the sheep. You know he has no fear whatsoever of the horses. I fell over him in the dark, so one of the mares must have run over him." The next realization felt like a gut punch. "A running horse could have killed him."

Dr. Brian said, "Come and look at the x-rays."

In a small adjoining room, we stood, staring intently at the light box that held images of my dog's shattered leg.

"The fracture compounded, as you can see with the exposed carpus bone," Dr. Brian said. "Although the break isn't smooth, it can be realigned, and should mend properly."

"What about the laceration?" I asked. "Will a cut with stitches heal in a cast?"

The veterinarian faced me squarely. My breath caught with his look of concern and trepidation.

Dr. Brian said, "I know Luke is your competition dog. I know how much he means to you. Although I can suture the skin and set the bone, my suggestion would be to take him to an orthopedic surgeon."

"Orthopedic surgeon," Mac said. "What would the difference in cost be?"

"Treatment by me and my staff here at the clinic would run right at a thousand dollars. With Dr. Dean, you're looking at forty-five hundred to five thousand."

From the moment I noticed Luke's horrific injury, my take-charge Queen aspect had reined efficiently. Stabilizing the leg, making the necessary calls, making sure Sharon could stay later and close up the barn. A sense of purpose had come over me as I held and soothed my dog during the drive. But this… an orthopedic surgeon, five thousand dollars? That amount might as well have been a million. For a second, I simply couldn't think.

"What would a surgeon do that you can't do here?" Mac asked.

"He would use metal rods and pins instead of a cast to stabilize the leg. There would be a greater chance that he would mend completely and return to work without pain. The suture site would be exposed and heal faster."

That settled it. Mending completely, work without pain… There was no way I would pick the option that *didn't* include those certainties for my boy.

After he got a temporary cast and a kiss on the head, we left my sleeping dog in the care of the hospital's night supervisor. We would return at seven-thirty in the morning to transport Luke to Doctor Dean and a prearranged surgery.

On the way home, a soft glow from the dash lights illuminated Mac as he turned to me, a mixture of relief and concern on his face. "How?"

He didn't need to finish the question. I knew what he meant. "I don't know. Sell Wynonna, take a second mortgage out on the farm?"

"Whatever it takes," Mac said.

"Whatever it takes."

Luke seemed to be completely unaffected by his new three-legged mode of mobility. The fractured leg, supported by an apparatus made of titanium rods and pins, had been drilled completely through the bone. The configuration held Luke's appendage directly out in front of his body and made me think of a rifle from outer space. Not to be deterred by any of these impediments, my dog would have taken off for the sheep with the slightest hint of a command.

During his six-week checkup, Dr. Dean announced, "The X-rays show the bone is completely mended. We can take the pins and rods out today. Give him two weeks to heal and gain strength before he works."

That afternoon, I lifted Luke from the backseat and placed him on the ground in front of the barn. He took a few gingerly steps and took off running directly to the pasture and the sheep grazing by the pond.

"Luke, here," I shouted. "Oh no you don't, young man."

I'm not quite sure how to describe profound disappointment on a dog's face. But I had no doubt at all that disappointment was what he felt.

In an instant, and with absolute clarity, I saw into Luke's soul. I saw past his beauty, past his human-like eyes, past my love of him and his for me. I saw his drive and passion. I saw the innate talent that fueled his heart and formed the foundation of his entire being.

I lost my breath as a truth washed over me. I wasn't a suitable owner for a dog with Luke's power and talent. His accident should have been avoided. Luke's injury would have never happened if I had followed one simple rule: Don't let your working dog roam unsupervised around livestock.

If I had released Luke's tether *after* I had watered the sheep, instead of before, my dog would have been with me. Luke's black form would have never been lying in the dark of night. He would never have been in the path of running horses. Luke might have been killed, or else harmed in such a way that would have prevented him from being the very thing that he was born to be: a herding dog.

My legs melted. I collapsed into a nearby chair. I would not, could not, ever be the handler Luke deserved. I simply wasn't the shepherdess my friends were.

After Luke's two weeks' recovery time, I made a call to Helen and mentally gripped my heart for the conversation with my husband.

Shafts of moonlight shone into the bedroom. Instead of lying down, I rested my back against the headboard and stared at leaf shadows dancing on the ceiling.

When Mac came in the room, I patted the headboard. "Sit. There's something we need to talk about."

As he pulled the covers back, he glanced at my face. "Uh-oh, you don't have that expression very often. You didn't knock another hole in the barn wall with the manure spreader, did you?"

"Honey, no. This is important."

"Didn't think there could be anything more important than a hole in the barn wall."

This time, he looked at me intently and raised his eyebrows. "That didn't get an irritated smirk... Now you're scaring me."

Finally, the words I had not been able to say all evening came tumbling out. "I'm giving Luke to Helen."

He stared. "There's no way you just said that."

"Yes, you heard me. If Luke is ever going to reach his fullest potential as a competitive dog, he needs to be with Helen."

"Woman, of all the crazy things you come up with, this is the most idiotic. Your brain must have turned to mush and dribbled out your ears."

The rehearsed reasons ran through my mind before I spoke. "This is not a decision made lightly. In fact, it's tearing me apart inside." I fought to keep my voice steady and blinked back threatening tears. "It's not good enough to simply accomplish something. Luke and I have accomplished something great, but... he deserves to be the best. And it's become very clear that he will not accomplish that with me. I can't even keep him safe!"

"This is not like you. You don't give up."

"I'm not giving up. I'm considering someone else before myself." I stared at the dancing leaves once more. "In Missouri, an errant sheep jumped into a five-foot water tank, and Luke followed. It took three people to get the huge sheep and my dog out. We were all soaking wet. In Arkansas, the sheep got past me, and Luke ran them around in the audience. People were hopping out of their lawn chairs and running out of the way. I don't care about placing, really, but he just can't keep having sheep-wrecks."

Then, something else became devastatingly clear, something I had felt but not wanted to acknowledge. "Luke knows when we have to leave the field without pinning the sheep. Maybe he feels my excitement on the rare occasion we get it done, or maybe he feels how let down I am when we don't. But, honey, I see the disappointment in his posture, in his eyes."

"I don't understand. You started at the bottom with horses. You know you can learn. You *have* learned... a lot. What about that second place at the Panhandle trial?"

"That had to be beginners' luck. We haven't had a smooth run since. Besides, dog training and horse training are different. Elaine trained my horse while I rode one of hers. That way, I had the skills and knowledge I needed to not confuse Nick, my first horse. Luke is ready now. He can't wait for me to learn to be a shepherdess."

"A what?"

"Helen is a shepherdess. She reads livestock. She knows what's going to happen before it does. When she works Luke at her house, he's a different dog. It's truly beautiful to watch. He likes her, and he would sleep by her bed.

"Helen is not only a good trial handler, she has a working ranch. Luke would have large herds of sheep and cattle. He would have a real job. Helen lost Bita, her national champion dog, a couple years ago. Her young dogs are nice, but not the caliber of Bita or Luke."

Mac's voice held a tone of suppressed anger. "What about all the money we spent on his leg? How can you just give that away? I think you've lost your mind."

"I know the money is an issue. The brood mare we sold will be a loss for the ranch, but, Mac, I have to do the best thing for my dog."

As if disbelief had just blended with comprehension, my husband sat straighter against the headboard. "This is not a discussion. I have no say in this. You've already made the arrangements, haven't you?"

What I saw in my husband's eyes made my stomach turn over. I couldn't speak. The silence between us was so profound it seemed loud, and I recognized something vital. The unshed tears in his eyes said it all. Luke occupied a place in my husband's heart as well as mine. I had been so wrapped up in my own grief, I hadn't taken Mac's love for Luke into consideration.

"Well?" came a soft voice that was far worse than a shout.

Finally, I found a way to whisper: "Helen's expecting him tomorrow."

The lamp on Mac's nightstand switched off. For the first time in fourteen years of sleeping in the same bed, the man slipped down into the covers and turned his back.

Chapter Twenty-Four

Our tiny ranch house served as a pacing track throughout the night. I was sure Mac wasn't sleeping, but he didn't say another word. Each time I lay down and tried to rest, I would look at his back and sense the hurt emanating from him. The feeling would send me out of bed and back to pacing.

During my fretful hours of wandering, I regretted making the decision about Luke before talking to my husband. I also ran the conversation with Helen through my mind.

My friend had been part of the herding world for years. She understood that dogs were often bought, sold, or traded. The reasons were numerous: personality conflict, different levels of talent, or even the fact that some handlers raised and trained puppies for the sole purpose of selling them. Helen had been surprised and honored by my offer of Luke. She hadn't argued with my reasoning. She did, however, set firm rules for the exchange.

She insisted that it would be an exchange. She would breed one of Bita's offspring to Luke, and I would have first choice of puppies. But, most importantly, once she competed with Luke, I *couldn't* change my mind.

"I've grown fond of Luke over the last year," Helen had said. "There's no doubt that it won't take long for him to own a piece of my heart. Even though I know you're not making this decision lightly, I will give you a little time to think after you leave him with me."

Around four in the morning, I thought about time. Helen was giving me time. Time to what? Change my mind? No amount of time could change the fact that when it came down to it, Luke deserved more than the ability I had. Someone who would protect him from hurt. He deserved the handler I could never be.

The need to sleep finally overcame my tormented mind, and I drifted off sometime before dawn. I awoke with the intention of putting words to the apology I had mentally formulated to my husband. I reached out for his shoulder, only to find his side of the bed empty.

"Mac, honey?"

No answer. I padded to the kitchen and looked out the back door. His truck was gone.

Anxiety quickened my heart rate. I knew my husband had gone to work early, but my rational mind couldn't seem to engage. My world was falling apart. It wasn't the first time I had caused someone important in my life to leave.

Barn sounds came from outside—feed buckets rattling, horses nickering, and the tractor starting. Sharon had arrived. But sounds that normally comforted me now sent me back to bed, where I curled up into a ball.

When I closed my eyes, I was seven years old again. Gripped suddenly by the loss and panic of waking up to find my mother's side of the bed empty. I could see My-Honey's kind face as she explained that my mother had tried to take her own life. I could see myself playing Camelot with my brothers while, alone in a hospital, my mother fought for her life.

My-Honey had loaded my brothers, me, and all our belongings into her powder-blue Chevy. As we headed across the country, she had turned to me with a smile that held a mixture of hope and pity. "It will take time for Eva to recover from the pills and alcohol. It'll be just us for a while. I'm so, so happy we'll be together. But I'll have to work double shifts. That means you"—my aunt placed her hand on mine—"will have to take care of your brothers."

As we traveled across the country, I left two vital parts of my very being behind: my mother and the little girl who played. After all, had I been a better daughter, my mother would have been with us.

I brushed away something cold on my forehead. Instead of leaving, it pressed harder. My eyes opened to a pair of eyes, a nose, and an intense look of *I need to go out.*

"Okay, let's go."

Luke and I went into the backyard, where I sat for a while, watching him. I knew we should be on the way to Helen's, but I just needed to be with him a little longer.

"Luke, here." I went to my knees as he approached. "We're going to Helen's today, and you'll stay with her. You'll have lots more sheep to work, and someone who will love you—never as much as I do, but Helen is the best person for you right now. Sweet, sweet handsome man, I hadn't known how much I needed you until you were here."

I closed my eyes and was once again at Mandy's when he peed on my leg. I smiled at him. I could see the sunset when he brought the sheep in for the first time. Then, I remembered that joyful winter morning in the hay meadow, and I knew I would carry that moment in my heart for eternity.

Thirty minutes later, we were headed south on Highway 75 toward McAlister and Helen Owens.

Chapter Twenty-Five

L uke knew exactly where he was when I made the last right turn onto Helen's drive. He whined and paced back and forth in excitement. Puddles of water glistened on the asphalt from an early morning rain. As I got out of the truck, I stood and watched the metallic swirling colors of oil. *That's it,* I thought. *I can be detached like that oil, just float on top and not let the ugly underneath show.*

As I let Luke out, Helen rode up on a chestnut gelding and dismounted.

"Had a couple missing calves this morning." She reached into her pocket for a treat and gave it, open-palmed, to the horse, then handed the bridle reins to a barn hand. "That wonderful animal gets through the trees better than a four-wheeler. Thanks, Brian." The man led the horse away. Helen looked intently at me. "I know you said you were sure, but are you?"

I pursed my lips and nodded. We walked toward the sheep's pasture.

"He'll have a good home here. I'm glad to have him. This dog will allow me to compete in classes I haven't been able to since Bita. She smiled. "He can also help bring the calves through the trees." Her green eyes grew serious. "There's a tristate qualifying trial in Waco, Texas, in a few days. If I call now, I can get Luke and me entered. So, I have to remind you... If I walk on the trial field with him, there's no going back." She knelt and roughed Luke around the collar. "This boy will be mine."

A pang went through my heart like something had seeped through the oil and pierced the core beneath. Before I could completely choke up, a movement behind Helen caught my eye. I glanced past her and down the gravel drive. Something brown paced back and forth. Goose flesh started at my feet and flew up my body.

Helen stood and looked in the same direction. "That's strange. I usually don't see her until dusk, and never around the sheep pens. She has a new litter of pups in the north woods. I heard them caterwauling last night."

The animal stopped and turned to look directly at us. "That's a coyote." I rubbed the skin on my arms.

"She won't come any closer." My friend noticed my goosebumps. "Clearly, she's got you bugged."

"That's not what I'm worried about." I brushed her off without taking my eyes off the animal. I couldn't believe it. Another coyote, and on the very day I was leaving Luke. Something more was happening here. I knew it.

"The trickster."

"What?" I finally met Helen's eyes. "What did you say?"

Helen grinned. "You know, the coyote. That's what he symbolizes." She turned in the direction of her house. "Come on. Bring Luke. Let's go see what that rascal animal means to you."

The long, homey room with its rich colors, crystals, drums, and rattles held the same fascination as it had the last time I entered.

Helen went to a mahogany case and picked up a purple book with gold lettering that read *Medicine Cards*. Tiny teeth marks marred the spine. She ran her fingers lovingly over the tattered and marked treasure. "I left this on the sofa when Bita was a puppy." She took in a breath. "Isn't it interesting how something that was a source of irritation at one time can be such a comfort now?" She handed me the book and a red velvet bag of cards.

"These are beautiful." I flipped through the deck. "Are these going to tell my fortune or something?

"No," Helen said. "The cards can act as a guide. You've heard of archetypes because of Chris."

I nodded.

"Well, not only do psychologists like him use archetypal patterns, but many of the indigenous cultures do also. Jamie Sams and David Carson compiled the observations of different animal personalities and traits into this book and companion cards."

"Hm… so, I'm not silly for getting the willies because I've been seeing a coyote at odd times during the last two years?"

"Just the opposite. I would call it intuitive."

I chuckled. "Intuitive, huh?"

Helen flipped through the book and found a page with a bat. "I dreamt three different times in one week that I died. When I became distraught over it, my boyfriend, Mark, brought out this deck of cards and told me to pick one. I chose the Bat out of fifty-two cards. This is what Bat signifies:

Sacred Bat… flew to me,
From the darkness of the cave.
Womb-like reflections, answers it gave.
Birth, death, rebirth, cycles of the whole…
Never-ending, just eclipsed.
The journey of the soul.

"Not only did the rebirth part make me feel much better, but a few months later we were married, and our relationship was certainly a journey of the soul."

"Wow, I'm a little nervous about what the book has to say." I shuffled through the cards and found the Coyote. The head of the animal was painted on a yellow shield. Hanging from the shield by twisted leather straps were feathers, a wishbone, an eagle claw holding a crystal, and a talisman. Brown fur tipped with black covered its face.

It had intense amber eyes that stared back at me. I felt like spiders were marching across my scalp.

> *Coyote... you devil*
> *You tricked me once more*
> *Must I sit and ponder,*
> *What you did it for?*

"I really don't understand the trick thing. All my reasons are black and white." I glanced at my dog lying beside the sofa.

"Read on," Helen said.

"*Coyote is sacred,*" I continued. "*The folly of his acts helps you to see your own foolishness and self-sabotage. If coyote is approaching you from the outside—*" I paused and looked up. "Well, he sure is doing that."

Helen nodded.

I went back to reading. "*Beware of this master of illusion. Coyote might pull you into the briar patch to pick berries. It will be a painful lesson if you follow him.*"

My eyes glossed over. Heat rose from my chest, and my ears felt as if they might burst into flame. "I don't feel well." I put my hand to my chest to stop the overwhelming burning. "Suddenly I feel like everything is on fire."

Helen gave a soft, silvery laugh. "Old wounds can trick your mind into believing all sorts of crazy things. Your temple bells are ringing with the truth of what you just read." My friend raised her eyebrow. "You can fool your mind, but your body has its own internal lie detector."

I held my hot ears in my hands. "You mean my body, or temple bells as you called them, are in conflict with my mind, like I'm living in some kind of illusion?"

A huge smile broke across Helen's face and she nodded. "Would you like some help?"

"Please," I whispered.

"Have you ever done any journey work or guided imagery meditation?"

I shook my head.

Helen stood and gathered items: a rattle, some amber liquid in a bottle, a drum. "What we are going to do is a mild form of hypnosis. I will take you into a type of trance state that, we hope, will let you see a time when you carried a wound or misconception."

"That's interesting," I said. "My husband, as you can imagine, wasn't exactly happy I'm doing this." I sent a wan smile toward Luke. "When I woke up this morning, Mac's side of the bed was empty. I felt an unreasonable sense of abandonment. The feeling triggered a memory of something that happened when I was a kid.

At seven, I used to sneak down to watch the horses at a rental stable. After my mom tried to take her own life, I felt that I was being punished for leaving my brothers."

I rubbed the scar on my forehead and went back further in time. "When I was five, I got hurt while running to see a litter of Border Collie puppies. I did something I had been warned not to do, and my grandmother lost her favorite rooster."

"Well, that tells me what we need to do. We need to go back further than this childhood. There has to be a reason those old memories are rearing their ugly heads now." Helen dipped her chin and peered over her glasses. "What do you say we go to the very beginning, to the lifetime of the original wound?"

"You mean we can see our past lives?" Suddenly, my heart lurched. Patting my chest, I said, "I think my temple bells just gonged."

I drew in a trembling breath. "I went to my first herding trial in California with my friend Ellie." In my mind, I saw Ellie's slender, dark-haired beauty. "She literally bribed me into going with her. I got so wrapped up in the herding, she joked that I must have been a sheep in a past life. She said it casually, but..." I shrugged. "I never really believed in multiple lifetimes."

Helen sighed. "Oh, sweetie, clearing old toxic imprints from past lives is the basic work of a shaman and many healing practitioners."

"Really?" I felt my eyes grow round.

"Yes, the foundation of a healer's work is the belief that nothing manifests in the physical body that doesn't begin in the emotional and spiritual realm. So, when old toxic imprints are ready to be healed, they show up as disease, accidents, profound sadness—all sorts of painful attention-getters. They often bring old memories to the surface."

"You mean there might be a reason for the crappy things in my life?" I waved my right hand, miming a rollercoaster.

"There's always a reason." Helen picked up two rattles and handed me one. "Before we get started, we need to make a sacred, safe container. We need to call in the archetypal directions and our angelic guides."

A feeling of doubt and trepidation made me want to run out the door with my dog and drive away—far, far away. But I had grown to love and trust Helen. I sucked in a breath and said, "Tell me what to do."

"We'll begin with the South. Face that way," she said as she pointed, "and rattle along with me."

Luke sat up at the intrusive noise but didn't move.

After Helen silenced her rattle, she said, "To the winds of the South, Serpent, wrap your coils of light around us. Help my sister to shed what does not serve her any longer—all at one time, like you shed your skin. Help her to shed her illusions and find the truth within."

Helen turned in the westerly direction and rattled again. I did the same.

"To the winds of the West, Jaguar, Otorongo, you who know the way across the rainbow bridge to the world of mystery. Help my sister to go beyond the fear of death. Help her to put to death the thoughts that do not serve her any longer. Help her to rebirth and recognize the luminous being she truly is."

As Helen turned to the North, I relaxed. All at once, I understood that the rattles signified a polite knock on an unseen spiritual door—a door that invited a symbol of each of the animal archetypes to join us.

"To the winds of the North," Helen continued. "Hummingbird, ancient ones, bring your wisdom. Help my sister to know that despite all, she has endurance. She has an internal guidance to her goals. Help my sister to drink, like you do, sweetly from the nectar of life.

To the winds of the East, Great Eagle, Great Condor, you have pushed my sister from the nest of comfort. Help her to fly wing-to-wing with you, to feel your updraft and soar. Show her to the place of life's highest possibilities."

As I understood the significance of each archetype and the power they instilled, I wanted to be them. No... I had to embody them. If I embodied them, I could find joy in Helen having Luke. I could revel in their accomplishments.

Helen placed her hand on the floor. "Mother Earth, Pachamama, thanks for all of our relations—the two-legged, the four-legged, the many-legged, the finned and the furred, the creepy crawlers, the stone people, and the plant people. May we all live in harmony and appreciation of one another. Thank you for your bounty that supplies our every need."

Helen rattled upward. "Grandmother Moon, Father Sky, our angels, our guides, thank you for your light as you shine it down upon my sister and me while we do this work. Thank you for allowing us to sing this song of life one more day." Helen laid her rattle down, a look of serenity on her face.

I stared at her in awe. "That was beautiful, really beautiful."

"Okay, we're almost ready." Helen picked up a remote and pushed a button. A quiet, rhythmic drum beat drifted through the room. "The drum will help you stay in the hypnotic state. In the ancient traditions, drums represent the circle of life and the heartbeat of Mother Earth."

My heart rate slowed in time with the soothing sound. I took a deep breath and when I exhaled, my entire body relaxed.

"We need to set an intention for your journey," Helen said. "We need to know what you wish to see, wish to heal."

What *did* I want to heal? Myself, I guessed. All I felt was uncertainty. "I don't know," I sighed. "I've come so far, accomplished so much, but I seem to hurt others by doing so. That's why it feels so important to think of Luke first now."

"Good," my friend said. "Your question can be: Why do I hurt others when I pursue my own dreams? Ask your guardian angels with your mind. Let them guide you, along with my voice."

I felt the butter-soft leather sofa embrace me as I lay down. Soon, I was able to visualize Helen's verbal images. I found myself walking down a path lined with pine trees and ferns, the ground soft with brown needles. Tattered bands of white clouds graced a blue sky. When she described a waterfall, I glanced to my right and walked closer to the sound of rushing water. A moist breeze kissed my face. The water careened downward into a crystal green pool where two deer were drinking.

How do I know I'm not making this up? my mind protested, but I couldn't seem to say it out loud. As I took in my surroundings, I could feel my eyes dart back and forth under closed lids.

"What does the ground look like under your feet?" Helen asked.

Her question shifted my internal vision. It took a moment to focus, but then I answered, "Green grass. About a foot tall. There are mountains all around. No, I'm on a mountain. I'm on the edge of a field surrounded by oak trees, and there are boulders covered with lichen."

"Are there any people there?"

As I cast my vision side to side, the wind brought cool, clean air, purer than I knew air could smell. "A boy." I inhaled, startled to actually see someone. "I can't make out his face. He's skinny."

"How's he dressed?"

"Um... tan breeches, worn, but not shabby. Tall brown boots, homespun tunic." I had to bring my breath back to verbalize what I saw next. "There's a rough leather thong hanging around his neck and a stamped piece of metal hanging from it... A whistle. He's standing in the center of a huge field. He's waiting for something, or someone. Wait... the ground's trembling." I turned toward the source of the disturbance. "Large, brown long-haired animals are charging into the field!"

"Is the boy afraid?"

"No, he seems excited. I can see him now. He has long, straight sand-colored hair. It's pulled back. Escaping strands are blowing all around his face. Yes, he's happy—he's running back and forth across the field and yipping."

The boy's happiness became mine. I forced myself to observe when what I wanted to do was run, jump, and share his joy. "There are animals here of some kind that might be sheep, but if they are, the beasts are bigger than anything I have ever seen. They have huge horns and thick, heavy fur of some kind. There must be fifty of them."

The boy picked up the piece of metal, put it in his mouth, and blew a loud, piercing warble. Within seconds, a black-and-white dog emerged from behind the sheep.

The animal looked like Luke. Instinctively, I reached to my chest, where my whistle always hung. The empty space felt hollow and bereft. My eyes glossed over. Then, silent tears overflowed, streaming down my temples and over my ears. I felt the pillow grow damp.

A shout brought my attention back to the boy. "Addie, that'll do Here… here, girl." The dog ran swiftly to the boy and sat in front of him. "Good girl, good girl. We got those blasted sheep back, now let's take them home." Something caught the boy's eye. As if it were my own, I felt concern wash over him. "What's the matter, girl?" the boy asked as he approached the ewe. "You're walking on three legs." He bent over to examine the leg.

A deep-chested growl caught my attention, and I glanced toward the perimeter of the flock. When I saw the source of the sound, I went cold. What had to be a giant mountain ram was careening straight for the boy.

"Watch out!" I shouted as fear flooded my mind, swift and horrible. "Why can't he hear me?" I cried. "He doesn't see him. The ram, he doesn't see him. I can't stop the charging ram. I can't get the boy to look up. No, no, nooo… The dog, the dog is running for the ram." The huge beast veered, lowered his head, and rammed the dog onto the ground. A piercing whine echoed through the field.

Bellowing like an angry bear, the animal focused on the boy once again. Before the youth could reach his fallen dog, the ram plowed into the boy's abdomen. Its powerful head and massive spiral horns sent the young shepherd flying fifteen feet into the air—air that no longer held a fresh, clean smell. A musty, acrid scent assaulted my nostrils.

The boy landed with a crack and a thud on the ground.

No longer concerned with the human, the ram joined the injured ewe and ushered her back to the flock.

"Help!" I shouted as I ran to the boy's side. "Someone help! There's too much blood."

The boy's head had hit an outcrop of stone. Long strands of sand-colored hair and red blood mingled with the lichen, making a jagged red line down the rock. My hand flowed completely through his shoulder as I tried to wake him.

I ran to the dog. A tiny amount of blood came from her nose and her tongue lolled from her mouth. A sickly, wrenching sensation clenched at my stomach. I knew that this boy loved this dog as much as life itself. My body went limp, and I fell to the ground. Empty, human-like eyes stared out into nowhere… Luke's eyes. For a moment, I simply couldn't find my breath.

A voice echoed in my head. "The choice is mine now." I jumped up to see a translucent vision of the boy standing beside me although his still, solid form lay on the ground.

For a long, confused moment, I stared at him. Then, I lifted my hand to see the same translucent appearance. As I stood transfixed, I slowly understood that neither of us were in corporeal form. The fear and horror were suddenly gone, as if we was watching a scene from a movie.

The etheric version of the boy was slightly taller than I was. We faced each other, and I looked up to find his eyes—deep blue eyes that were lit from the same light as my soul. Instantly, I understood that we were different versions of the same heart.

"I snuck out before dawn this morning to bring the herd down from the summer meadows. I wanted to have them back before noon so I could run my horse in the fair races this afternoon."

I gave an internal chuckle in appreciation, then pointed to the form on the ground. "What happens if he lives?"

"As horrible as it seems now," he said, "this experience is vital to the evolution of our soul."

Understanding washed over me. "What happens next affects every lifetime up to and including this one." I placed my hand on my chest. For the briefest moment, I wanted to plead with him to transition, to let death take him so he would not suffer through the loss of his dog.

Although I hadn't spoken out loud, he smiled in understanding. "Yes, it would be much less painful to simply join our soul parts and let Ma and Da carry the burden of loss. But the pain of losing a child is not part of their journey."

From a distance, a male voice boomed through the field. "Jamie!" Louder, the man shouted, "Jamie!" A large red-haired man prodded the mammoth sheep out of his path with a long staff. "Addie." The man sprinted to the dog on the ground. "Addie... girl." The hopeful expression on his face fell into instant grief. With a hand so large it covered the dog's black-and-white head, he gently closed her eyes. "You were a great dog," he whispered. Then, he stood and cast a look around the meadow.

In a few long, lumbering strides, he knelt by the sprawling form of the shepherd boy. "Jamie!"

The youth's eyelids fluttered. "Da."

I snapped my head toward luminous form of boy beside me.

He smiled knowingly, nodded, and was gone.

"Thank the Gods," the man said.

"Da," the boy said. "Da, I'm so stupid."

"Shush," the man whispered. "You've hit your head. Let me see." He slipped an arm around Jamie's shoulders and lifted. Then his free hand parted the tangled blond hair and examined his scalp. "Well, you're going to have a goose egg and need sewing up, but it looks worse than it is. Let me help you up."

As Jamie tried to stand, he gasped, and his arms went to his side. "I think I might have some cracked ribs."

"Take your time, boy." His father sat on the ground beside him. "What happened?"

"The ram, Da. I was checking a ewe's leg, and the ram came out of nowhere."

"Why did you come out here alone? How many times have I told you not to turn your back on a ram?" The man's deep, raspy voice emphasized his growing anger. "Your idiocy could have cost us the entire herd, not to mention what your death would have done to your mother. Vicious doesn't describe the protectiveness of a ram in rutting season. You know that."

"I'm sorry, Da." Then his eyes grew round in sudden panic. "Addie, where's Addie?"

The man's ruddy face softened, and he shook his head slowly, looking in the direction of the still, black-and-white form.

"Addie," Jamie sobbed, and managed a scooting crawl on his elbows over to his dog. "Da... Addie... oh, Da, it's my fault."

For the first time, I heard the wailing lament of a heart shattered by grief and loss. I heard a soul crying out in protest so strongly that every cell in his body seemed to weep.

A loud, rapid drum beat startled me. Someone shouted *Naomi* in a panicked tone.

"Helen?" In an instant, my eyes flew open.

"You just scared ten years of life from me, girl." She set the wooden drum down and turned off the CD player. "I've never lost control, never lost touch with anyone during a past-life journey. You just took off on your own."

Disoriented, I sat on the edge of the sofa. In a second of panic, I looked down at Luke, placed one hand on my chest and one on my dog, and breathed, "He's alive."

Helen glanced at Luke and said, "That must have been pretty traumatic."

"I don't know where to start. Traumatic might be an understatement. I understand so much now—my *déjà vu* around herding and sheep, my love of mountains, and my connection to farm life." I took a deep breath. "Also, why I'm drawn to primarily male hobbies and jobs."

I sucked in a breath, and for several long moments my heart and mind were at war. Then I asked, "I know now that Luke has been with me lifetime after lifetime. Does that mean that no matter what, we belong together?" I shook my head. "No! I saw one of my precious boy's deaths. I will not be a cause of another one."

"That might..." Helen began.

A cold resolve placed itself firmly in my belly. "Helen, I think what I just witnessed was the reason Luke and I were led to you. It confirms my decision. You will care for him with the wisdom of experience. You will allow him to live in the ranching world he was born to be a part of." Then, I lied to my friend as I whispered, "I might have another dog one day."

Helen softly replied, "This is not the outcome I had hoped for. Naomi, give yourself time to process what you saw, what you felt. Look for the patterns in the memories. To survive childhood trauma, we build tough walls around ourselves, around our hearts. Think about what those walls could be, and please don't be afraid to let them fall."

"Thank you. I will." I hugged Helen, smiled at Luke, gathered up every ounce of courage I had, and walked out the door.

Chapter Twenty-Six

O nce on the highway, I wondered about the tragic vision, about my memory from the morning. Did they link together somehow? I had hoped working with Helen would have helped ease the pain of leaving Luke, but I only felt heartsick—if heartsick is, in fact, when your heart and your stomach and your insides feel empty and hollow and aching.

When I pulled onto the ranch parking lot, the meanings in my head were all jumbled up with my heart. I couldn't escape the turmoil.

To avoid speaking to anyone, I parked beside Mac's truck and strolled around the barn and out to the sheep pen.

I marveled at the differences in my doll-like miniature Cheviot sheep and what must have been Highland Scottish sheep.

"I really didn't think you'd do it."

My body stiffened at Mac's voice. For a long moment, I stood in judicial silence and waited for an indication of my husband's mood. When he didn't say anything further, I said, "These ewes have been birthing twins and triplets. If we let the spring lambs mature, we can sell *all* the sheep. There's no need to keep them any longer. The proceeds will almost replace the broodmare we sold."

"If that's what you want to do." His face held a benign expression, as if he wasn't sure what to say. Finally, he cleared his throat and said,

"Helen called to see if you made it home okay. I told her your truck was here. She said you had quite a day."

"Too much to think about, too much to process. I'm really not ready to talk about it."

"Okay, I get it. You might call Helen. I think she's concerned."

"Well, evidently you're not concerned." It felt as if my emotions had their own language and no one to translate. I was angry that Mac hadn't asked how I was. I felt lost. I didn't know what to do without planning Luke's work schedule. I felt empty, no longer a whole being. A part of me had been left behind with my friend. Turning my back on Mac, I went to the phone and called Helen.

"He kept looking for you," Helen said. "We went to the south pasture and worked. It took a while to fully have his attention since you weren't there. But, wow, once he dialed in, he was amazing."

My heart constricted, and I took a moment to speak. "That's why you have him."

"Are you really okay with this? I've bought trained dogs before, but this is different. That's why I offered to help you."

"Helen, enjoy your new dog. Go accomplish great and wonderful things. If you two place high enough, you'll gain points to qualify for the tristate finals—something I never could've done. I'll be fine." In that instant, the conflict within abated, and I knew I would be. I knew I would one day revel in seeing Luke's talent fully realized.

"Before I hang up, though," Helen paused. "Is there some strife still going on between you and Bart?"

That dark, broody, bitter man was the last person I thought Helen would mention. Chuckling, I said, "I don't know what it is between me and Bart. I guess strife is as good a word as any. Why?"

"He was filling in for Marsha, the show secretary, when I called to enter the trial. The second I gave my name as handler for Luke, I swear, the man laughed like a demented hyena."

I scowled. "That snake has told me from the beginning that he thought my dog was too good for me. He must be feeling really smug about that now."

"Huh. I don't know about that. But I did agree to take Luke. You know I will love and care for that boy as you would. Colby and her dogs are riding with Luke and me to Waco Thursday morning. If I run him and place high enough to qualify, I'll send in his transfer papers so he'll be in my name."

I steeled my nerves, steeled my heart, steadied my voice, and said, "I know you want the best. I do too, so... drive safely, do good... have a great time. Bye, Helen."

"Bye, Naomi."

Once the line was dead, I whispered, "Bye, my handsome man."

The next day, every chore, every horse I rode, every thought, contained an image of Luke. I could feel his happy human-like eyes following my movements as I worked in the barn. I couldn't shake the urge to reach down and pet him or talk to him. The hollow aching of my insides, of my heart, would not ease. Finally, desperation sent me out to the pond dam. Out to where I knew the coyote lived.

The canopy of willow leaves hung perfectly still in the cool air. The setting sun cast a golden twilight sheen across the water. Tiny perch broke the surface to feed on evening bugs.

Sitting on the ground with my knees pulled to my chest, I thought of Helen's last words: "Look for the patterns."

The feeling of a presence beside me drew my attention. As I turned, the Scottish boy Jamie slowly coalesced into a translucent form. His deep-blue eyes danced, and long, sandy-blond hair hung to his shoulders. His grin reminded me of a mischievous teenager. The hand-stamped whistle hung against his homespun wool shirt.

"I don't know what's weirder," I gasped as shivers ran down my spine, "that I see you, or that I can talk to you?"

"People talk to themselves all the time. I came to help." His grin grew bigger. "Call it self-help."

I choked on a chuckle. "Okay, help."

"Your friend was correct about looking at the patterns in your life. Let's start from now and work backwards. Let your mind see, let your body feel the events that cause you such sadness, such remorse and guilt."

"That's a long list. I've been thoughtless most of my life."

"I need to work on patience." He shrugged. "So, we can both get better at something. Proceed. Take all the time you need."

I closed my eyes. I could see Luke clearly. I could feel the withering pain in my gut at the sight of his foot dangling with a bone protruding. That memory triggered others, times when I had hurt my mother and my brothers.

My father's angry face loomed over me at age five. I held my breath and trembled. I could feel the pain in my head and hear him shout, "It's your fault your grandmother lost her favorite rooster!"

In an instant, I saw my five-year-old self on the ground in the chicken pen, wrapped in my mother's arms. She held a dish towel to my forehead. Something was off. The memory expanded somehow.

To my surprise, my grandmother had been the one to pull the flapping black-and-red rooster off my body. "Please don't do this, Robert." My grandmother stepped back away from my father.

"Please," my mother begged.

That's when the short blond man stepped forward, jerked the bird out of my grandmother's embrace, and viciously slung the rooster's body around until his head snapped completely off.

Along with that final vision came the realization that my father had killed my grandmother's bird out of malice and anger.

"Two things happened on that day," Jamie said, "vastly important evolutionary things. First, you were blamed for something that someone else did out of temper. But, most importantly, you, as a tiny girl, felt the guilt so profoundly that you've carried it around as a stain on your heart, as a stain on your very being."

I thought of the journey Helen had guided me through, and now I understood. "It began during my lifetime as you." My heart thudded. "The guilt of Addie's death."

The Scottish boy smiled and nodded. "There's a part of everyone's soul that strives for wholeness, strives for balance, strives to be clear of emotional stains that sabotage your dreams. Those stains can act as magnets drawing the same emotions over and over until they are finally addressed and healed. So really it's all good, all a blessing."

"This is crazy. Talking to you is crazy. I'm listening to a long-dead shepherd boy who's supposed to be *me*."

"Who would you rather listen to?" He grinned. "A rugged, good-looking, all-wise teenage part of your soul, or the middle-aged sad lady who's eaten up with guilt and doesn't believe she's worthy of her dog?" He tilted his forehead toward me and stared into my eyes.

"You want me to believe that I drew those crappy experiences to myself as some part of an evolutionary journey, and I should be happy about it?" My voice went up an octave. "I did give my dog away, for pity's sake... How's my shattered heart a good thing?"

"Let me ask you this. Would you have ever sought the help of someone like Helen if you weren't caught up in an illusion that justified your pain?"

I snapped my head toward him. "Illusion?"

Something deep and powerful stirred as a slow wave of realization finally surfaced. The coyote, the brambles of illusion—I tricked myself into believing I didn't deserve Luke, that I wasn't good enough for him. I made up a story that something lacking in me caused others to be hurt.

My mind reeled as the patterns fell into place. "I've found a way to blame myself for tragedies all my life." I glanced at Jamie. "Other lifetimes, too?"

He nodded and tented his fingers. "It's time to go forward, my dear soul. Forward into a journey of really learning who you are as a spirit."

"This is bigger than this lifetime. This is healing the part of me that's eternal."

In the span of a heartbeat, the air around me shimmered. Jamie no longer sat beside me. The boy's translucent presence floated above the pond. As he smiled, a crystalline glow lit up his entire form and expanded into a brilliant rainbow of colors.

The willow leaves swayed in a light breeze. Jamie said, "Listen to your heart. Listen to the whispers in the wind. Listen to the rivers and the earth and the animals."

As the last rays of the sun said goodbye, so did Jamie's ethereal presence.

Chapter Twenty-Seven

The lights were on in the house. Mac was home. Could I tell him what I had just experienced? Would he understand, or think I had gone completely mad? I hadn't spoken much to my husband in the last two days. I decided it was best to keep Jamie to myself.

"I brought Chinese," he said. "I have some paperwork to do, then I'm going to bed."

"Okay." After an uncomfortable silent meal, I went to the barn to finish the night chores.

Bootsie Myrtle followed me up and down the aisles, meowing insistently. When finished, I picked her up and sat down on a bench in the front of the barn. Stars shone brightly in the velvet darkness. Crickets chirped, and the coyote yowled her song. "I'm too late," I shouted toward the sound. "I understood your illusion too late."

I held Bootsie to my chest, comforted by the vibration of loud purring. "You miss him too, huh? Well, sweetie, Luke's in Waco, Texas, being a fantastic herding dog for Helen." The cat rubbed her cheek against mine. I ran my fingers through her long gray fur. "I see the reasons for the heartbreaks. I can appreciate them, even, for the lesson I learned… But dang!"

I let out a long sigh. Suddenly, joyful dampness filled my eyes. I felt it. I had it. Like a spark igniting a fire, I glowed with it. I felt a profound and inexplicable happiness for my friend and the dog that would always hold a piece of my heart.

Seven hours later at one o'clock in the morning, I heard, *Come and get me!* I sat bolt upright in bed. *Mom, come and get me!* I blinked several times. The words ricocheted in my head. Where did they come from?

*Mom, Mom...*This time, the words touched my heart like a silent plea.

Listen. Jamie had told me to listen.

Prickles ran over my scalp. Suddenly, I knew how a dog's back must feel when the hair stands straight up. "Luke?"

Mom, Mom, come and get me! My ears sang with a rush of blood and excitement.

"Luke, I'm on my way."

My fingers shook as I dialed Helen's cell.

"The party you are trying to reach is not taking calls at this time." I listened to the recording ten times before I remembered that the Waco trial grounds had no cell service. Helen must be sleeping in her camper.

"Honey, wake up." I shook Mac's shoulder, my pounding heart making my voice shake with intensity. "Honey, we have to go. Wake up."

Mac shot straight up in bed. "Is a horse sick? Is the trailer hooked up?" He rubbed his eyes and searched for his jeans.

"No, we're going to Waco, Texas."

My husband stopped after one bare foot made it through the jeans leg. He sat on the bed. "Why are you waking me up in the middle of the night to go to Waco?" His jeans landed on the floor.

My mouth opened to say the words, "Luke's calling me," but I snapped it shut. My husband would have declared me crazy and gone back to bed. I thought, *I am crazy*. But the feeling of urgency overtook my common sense. I said, "Luke and Helen are there."

"That doesn't answer my question. I'm not driving to Waco for you to watch someone else run your dog."

"No! I'm competing with my dog... *my dog.* I have to be there before eight." I picked up his jeans and pushed them toward him. "Put these on. I'll explain on the way. I haven't been to sleep. Just thinking, just sorting things out in my head, and I need to get Luke. Hurry!"

"Why don't you simply call Helen and tell her you've changed your mind? You said she gave you some time, so get him when she gets back." He sat on the edge of the bed with his jeans in his hands. "I can't take all this yo-yo stuff, Naomi. You haven't said three words in two days, and now you want me to drive you to Waco on some silly mission to get a dog you gave away. I'm going back to sleep."

"Please. I tried to call Helen, but there's no cell service at the trial grounds. Come on, I'll explain on the way. Mac, if I'm not in time, I'll lose him forever. If Helen competes with him, I can't have him back. Please, it's six hours to Waco. It's one o'clock now."

My husband lay down and pulled up the covers.

"Fine," I blurted. "I'll see you Sunday sometime." I dressed, grabbed my whistle and lanyard from the dresser, and placed it around my neck. Then I grabbed a small bag and stuffed some clothes in. The feeling of urgency grew stronger by the minute. I sprinted into the barn, wrote a note to Sharon, and gathered a few supplies: my crook, a tether chain, a crate, and a long horse line.

I sighed when I saw Mac behind the steering wheel of the truck.

"You have some explaining to do," he said after I loaded Luke's necessities in the backseat and sat down.

Nodding, I said, "I do. Helen has no way of knowing I changed my mind." *No way of knowing Luke is calling me.*

All through the night, our headlights cut a path through the darkness and bugs pelted the windshield. I poured out the long-forgotten and newly excavated memories. I told him about seeing the patterns, about understanding the reasons for the heartaches.

Mac sat silent as a shadow. After shutting off the engine at a fueling station, he shifted in his seat and put his arm across the back of my seat.

His eyes had an expression so kind it caught me off guard. He had no pity in his china-blue orbs. No judgment. He didn't collude with the tragic stories. He simply flashed a generous smile that lit his entire face and said, "We'd better hurry if we're going to get your boy."

My husband operated the diesel pump while I went inside for a pit stop and coffee, lots of coffee, and packaged snacks.

"Just the coffee," Mac said. "Food makes me sleepy."

For me, quite the opposite was true. I needed something to calm the jittery feeling in my stomach. The longer we drove, the more certain I became that Luke was, in fact, calling for me. Driven by nervous energy, I gobbled two packages of much-loved but always forbidden Ding Dongs. The chocolate seemed to connect my emotions and my brain. It was time to go on with the rest of my story.

Mac and I had never spoken about reincarnation or anything remotely related to the subject. He might call me insane, and our moment of kind understanding would be lost. So, I gathered my words together carefully before I released them, then poured out the harrowing past-life experience with the boy Jamie, Addie the Border Collie, and the Scottish Highlands. Then, I went on to my experience on the pond dam.

"My great aunt believed in the sort of things you're talking about. She passed a long time ago. My mother thought she was crazy, but I thought she was fascinating and wise."

Relief flooded through me, and I relaxed back into the seat. "You don't think I'm delusional or silly?"

"A little silly, maybe." He lifted a brow.

I grinned. My husband's humor had returned.

Again, Mac was silent. We drove on as the sun followed the moon across the sky. Pinks and blues lit up the cloudy horizon. Finally, he said, "I suppose it makes sense. I certainly understand some of your quirks. I understand why no matter what you accomplish, it never seems good enough to you."

For the briefest of moments, I basked in my husband's kindness and the beauty of the sky. I could see Luke's face, feel his silky fur as I wrapped my arms around him.

My eyes flashed on a road sign, and suddenly I couldn't breathe, couldn't think. My stomach roiled, and I thought I might have to pull over and upchuck Ding Dongs. The mileage marker had to be wrong, or something was wrong with my eyes. I was just tired, that was it. The digital clock on the dash glowed six forty-five as the truck sped closer to the sign that read *Waco: 120 miles.* After Waco, we had more miles of winding roads to the trial grounds by the river.

"Mac, you have to drive faster. Please, you have to drive faster." During all the explanations, all the intensity of our journey, I had not shed a tear. Now, a silent river streamed down my cheeks. There would be no possible way for us to arrive before eight. I could feel Luke slipping away from me with every distant mile.

Two hours later, we saw signs for the event.

I pointed east as we arrived. "We parked in a pasture at the end of that gravel road last time I was here." Several vehicles parked on the narrow shoulder for at least a half mile. A yellow wooden barrier blocked the road entrance. "Stop, let me out. You'll have to turn around and park behind these trucks."

"Okay, go," Mac said. "I'll find a place… Go." He waved toward the gravel road.

Desperation drove me out of the truck, and my feet hit the ground running. At first, there were only puddles along the gravel, but it was soon clear that a tributary or a creek must have flooded its banks. A thirty-foot-wide river of rushing water flowed across the road. I plowed straight into it, splashing through the knee-high torrent. Then, I darted around the trucks and cars in the parking area. Spotting Helen's silver truck and camper, I ran to them. No one was there. I spun, searching.

"That has to feel better," I heard a familiar voice say, drawing my sight toward a line of trees.

Luke stood for a very long time, his leg hiked on an ash tree.

My breath vanished from my chest for several heartbeats. Sweat ran down my temples despite the chill in the air. My jeans were soaked to the thigh and water sloshed inside my boots.

Luke happily trotted to Helen, who smiled and ran a hand down his back in affection.

As I witnessed the casual intimacy between the two, I felt lost in a swirling vertigo. Had I actually heard Luke calling to me? Or had that been something my heart made up because I couldn't let go of my wonderful dog? Once again, my mind and emotions were at war.

But then I noticed something else: Luke's bounce and Helen's cheerful effervescence. They had done well. It was clear as day from their body language. I was too late.

I choked on something that could have been a sob or a laugh, and a hard smile grew across my face. They had been victorious. And isn't that what I wanted? For Luke and my friend to be happy and successful.

Helen *was* the right person for Luke.

I had to let go.

I turned away from them, ready to sprint. If I hurried, I could catch Mac before he waded through the water that blocked the road. But before I could move, I heard a shout.

"Naomi, stop!"

My feet felt rooted to the ground, but I couldn't face the voice. I couldn't turn and allow the tenuous hold I had on my new reality to snap. "It's okay, Helen." I squeezed my eyes shut. "I know I'm too late. When you get home, I want to hear all about your run." My feet moved to carry me in the direction of my husband.

"No!" Helen shouted.

A piercing whine cut through the air.

I glanced around just in time to see Luke lunge at the end of Helen's leash. His eyes were bright, gazing into my soul the way he always did. But this time it was different. I had severed the magnetism between us, and he was straining to reconnect it. To tell me I had been right to listen to him. I had been right to come for him.

I was running before I could stop myself.

Helen must have unleashed Luke's collar because soon he was

running to meet me, his eyes shining, his legs barely touching the wet ground. I fell to my knees and let my dog collide with my arms, wrapping them around his wriggling form.

Laughter bubbled under Helen's words. "No, you're not too late. Flooding from heavy rains yesterday evening stranded some of us in, and others out. The trial's been postponed until noon."

Joy beamed from my friend's eyes, as though she could see the change in me. She could see that I had made it through the brambles of illusion that had held me trapped in pain for so long. "You're okay?" she said.

I smiled and nodded. "You knew... You knew I would work it out for myself and I would come for him."

"Um, let's say I hoped. Let's say I knew you had the strength and the will to face the pain of the past and let it become something to grow from."

"But Luke... you... the trial..." I felt my face scrunch into pure misery.

"I want what you want, the best thing for your dog. It's time to go change the handler's name to the one that should have been there all along... yours, my dear friend."

I held on to my dog for several long moments. "I'm here, sweetheart. I will never let you go. You are mine and always will be."

After trudging across the field, we reached the sign-in table, out of breath and exultant.

When I told Marsha, the show secretary, what I wanted, she tucked her black curl behind her ear. "You're outside the required time needed to change the handler's names by a hair, but for you..." She looked at my pleading face and smiled. We can make an exception, just this once. Forty-two dogs are entered. You're fifth to run."

She turned as a motion caught her attention. "Bart!" she shouted toward the back of a tall man in a black cowboy hat striding away. "Bart, I thought you were going to help me with the score sheets!"

"Do it yourself!" he shouted back.

Colby and my disheveled husband joined us at the sign-in table.

"All set?" Mac asked.

I nodded.

"You don't look so happy," Colby said.

Still focused on the retreating man, I said, "He's angry I showed up. I don't get it. Whenever I run Luke, he's always looming in that black hat. I've tried to talk to him, but it never goes well."

Marsha's eyes narrowed. "Come to think about it, Bart's been in a great mood since we got here. He was laughing and joking last night at dinner. I don't know what's gotten into him."

I felt as if a family of spiders were dancing the Macarena on my scalp. "Oh, sweet Sherlock. I can't stand this any longer. That man is going to tell me why he hates me."

"Just let him be," Colby grabbed my arm as I turned to go after him.

"Nope, this ends right here." I took off at a brisk walk, all the while grumbling to myself, *You're about to come tumbling off know-it-all-hill, mister.* By the time I cleared the trees Bart was watering his dogs, engrossed in his own tirade of grumbling.

"You wasted your time coming to Waco," Bart said. Somehow, he knew it was me coming up behind him. Turning, he glared. "That dog is in the right hands with Helen. You don't have the chops or the talent to deserve an animal like him."

The bitterness in his voice stopped me short. It stopped my brain from making a cohesive thought. My head felt like someone had dumped in Scrabble tiles. I couldn't form a word.

I simply stood there. We were so close, my face was eye to eye with the buttons on his starched black shirt. That's when one single word echoed like chimes through my entire body: *deserve.* He said I didn't deserve Luke.

Then two more words aligned themselves in my mind; I could see them with crystal clarity. I lifted my head to look past the stiff-tight-jaw, past the black intricately trimmed goatee, and said, "Thank you."

His dark brows lifted in question.

"The only person who needs to feel I deserve my dog is me. A part of me believed the snide comments, believed the antagonistic jibes you threw at me whenever you had the chance. So, I truly, and humbly, thank you."

Bart stepped away, his shoulders sagging, jaw softening. He seemed, for once, at a loss for words.

"I know unequivocally that I not only deserve Luke; I know that all of this between us has a purpose. I found mine. I hope you find yours." I spun on a heel and went to get my dog ready.

Chapter Twenty-Eight

An eagle floated circles across a vivid blue sky. Luke and I stood at the handler's post, looking out at the lush green five-acre trial field. Gentle hills added slopes and difficulty to the competition grounds. Strategically placed white portable fence panels would help demonstrate a dog's livestock maneuvering capabilities. The distant mountain peaks somehow offered a magnificent presence of protection, of comfort, of home.

Yes, I felt as if I had gone home. I felt one with the sky, with the eagle, with the mountains, but most of all, with my dog. A fierce, joyous serenity of purpose suffused with the feeling of wholeness held me steady as I stood next to Luke.

Once four white, wooly sheep had settled in the distance, I said, *"Away to me, my love."*

Luke took off from my right side in a wide counterclockwise arc. My dog and the sheep progressed perfectly through the lift and fetch maneuvers. During the drive portion, I lost sight of all five animals behind a hill, only to have them emerge headed in the wrong direction.

My whistle suddenly felt heavier, more crudely formed in my mouth. It seemed as if I had grown taller. An image of the Scottish boy Jamie flashed through my mind, and I knew without a doubt that I had the heart and the instinct of a shepherd, that he and I were one and had been all along. I emitted a quick bobwhite sound. Within a matter of seconds, Luke had the sheep heading straight for the pen enclosure that marked the end of our run.

And I knew something else. That the childlike, playful part of myself had returned. It didn't matter how we placed that day. Luke was doing what he loved, and we were doing it together.

After I closed the gate to contain the four sheep, I stood frozen in a moment of amazement at our accomplishment. Luke brushed my jeans, as if to say, *Hey, I'm not done.*

"Oh, right." I opened the gate. Luke walked in quietly, maneuvered behind the animals, and guided them to the holding area.

My dog ran to me as I walked toward the gallery of spectators. He whirled and hopped and danced around my legs.

"You were wonderful!" I gasped as I dropped to my knees and wrapped my arms around him. With the warmth of his body came a sense of completeness that spread to my bones and heart.

I stood, raised my crook high above me, leapt up into the air, and let out a loud shriek as the joy of a shepherd passed down through the ages.

Before I walked three steps, I found myself embraced by my crying, laughing husband and friends.

Epilogue

"You're here for him." I ran my hand down Luke's black, sun-warmed fur.

The Scottish boy's soft blue eyes glanced in my dog's direction, and he nodded. Long, sandy-blond hair escaped from a plait. He still wore the hand-stamped whistle.

I hadn't seen or felt him since that day at the pond dam.

Squeezing my eyes shut, I wrapped my arms around my knees and rocked back and forth on the ground. Silent tears streamed down my cheeks. "We've had twelve amazing years together, five of them traveling around the country herding critters. We made a pretty good team. This dog, this brilliant animal, changed people's lives."

Jamie sat in front of me cross-legged. "What about you?" he asked.

"Winning that first blue ribbon in Waco didn't feel like I thought it would. Oh yes, I was certainly proud of it—proud of Luke. But when I look back, every emotion building up to that moment had its place: the sorrow, the pain, the joy. Every bit of it had a purpose, but they were all only fleeting states of mind. None of it reflected who I truly was. Winning, losing, happy, or sad didn't define me." I took in a deep breath and smiled. "I know now that my parents were only doing the best they knew how when I was a child. I can thank them profoundly for who they were. I wouldn't change a single minute.

Bart and I became friends. He and Mac are even buddies. Helen now teaches classes on the medicine men and women's art of energetic healing. Funny, Bart was her first client after me. She helped him physically and emotionally. It was a good day when he came to tell me thank you. It made my heart happy."

Jamie flashed the grin I remembered and glanced down at Luke.

My eyes followed his. "With this dog, I began a journey I could never have expected, could never have come close to dreaming about or wishing for. Because of him, I studied animal communication with the best teachers, became a healer with my own practice. I serve the animals as a voice, as a link between them and their humans."

I felt my lips form into smile. "Because I believed in my connection with you, because I listened to your—self-help," my smile grew wider, "I listened when I heard animals that have traveled the rainbow bridge." I tingled all over with the magnitude of my next statement. "I would beg for one more minute, one more day, one more year, but I know Luke's job in this body is done. I know the earth is reclaiming what has been borrowed, and his spirit will eternally be alive and connected to me."

"Do you remember?" Jamie asked. "My-Honey's comment about someone's name being a mirror into their soul."

"Yes!" I brightened. "Luke. I never looked up what his name means."

Jamie's blue eyes danced. "LUKE, *Bringer of Light*."

I nodded, "Fitting—perfect—I should have known."

"He has two requests," I said. I glanced at Luke and stroked between his ears. "First: make a diary of our journey together. Second: share his experience of today. I'm to put down in words, his thoughts, feelings, and images of the day he passes. He wants to help others."

It was Jamie's turn to nod, his smile a confirmation.

Mac's truck and Doctor Brian's car pulled into the drive at the same time. Jamie stood alongside us with a dog I recognized as Addie. I pulled Luke into my lap, ran my hands through his coat, and hugged him tight one last time.

Then I looked up at the clear blue November sky, felt the warm breeze on my cheeks, and vowed to honor his requests.

Luke Speaks

*M*y mom, Naomi, wakes to find me lying in a pool of bloody urine. In one single moment, all her fret and doubt vanishes.

"No, no, no! Oh God, I'm not ready. I don't know how to do this without you," Mom chokes out.

She holds my head in her hands, and our eyes meet. I'm so ready, I tell her silently, knowing she'll understand.

Mom lays down clean towels and helps me out of the foul-smelling mess. I stand there shaking, my hips too unstable to move on the slippery floor.

"Oh, Luke, my handsome man, I can't make this call. I can't," she cries. A part of her is trying with all her might to avoid the finality that call will bring.

Mom finishes wiping the floor and calls Dr. Brian, the veterinarian. After a long professional relationship, the two have become friends. He knows the only event that could leave my mom holding back sobs and unable to speak would be my passing. After a few moments of helpless head shaking, Mom squeaks, "Yes," and then, "2:30 is okay."

Watching her clean up both me and the green-painted cement floor, I feel her sense of lucid detachment, like clouds floating lazily above her body, allowing her to do what is necessary... when what she would really like to do is fall into a puddle of blubbering tears.

But there is no time for that. I really need to go out to pee.

My name is Luke, and I'm a Border Collie. Although I'm black and white with the common markings—white down my face, white mane, white tip on my tail—I am unique in that my eyes are like a human's, with white showing around my brown pupils. It takes a minute for people to recognize what's different about them. My eyes might be what gave me my awesome sheep-moving power. I'm one of the best sheep dogs around. The only thing I love more than working sheep is my mom, though Dad comes pretty close.

Dream Maker Ranch is my home. My job is to announce the arrival of anyone human and know the whereabouts of anything with wool. (Except for Lee—that llama has an overinflated ego and only swats at me when I come up behind him.)

Mom and I have been together almost twenty-four/seven for twelve years. I didn't need the light jingle of her always-present spurs to know where she was. We were drawn together like the internal guidance system of a homing pigeon.

Finally, Mom notices my head on her leg and the panic on my face. I thought she'd never help me outside.

Despite the way it might look, I'm not dying today. That might sound weird, but I am actually letting the part of myself that is borrowed from the earth to return to where it came from. Once my heart stops beating, it will be like taking off a strikingly handsome old coat. (Mom always calls me her handsome man.)

My spirit, the part of me that is eternal, will still be very much alive. In fact, my spirit has been detaching for days, knowing it is time to leave this very painful body—this body that can no longer run in the hay meadow or bring the sheep in at night. The physical body can suffer, but the spirit does not.

I came to the earth plane fully evolved, magnificently conscious in crystalline expression with the single purpose of helping my mom evolve, grow, and learn.

The day is sunny and warm, unusual for mid-November. It feels so nice to lie on the sun-warmed grass. Mom is sitting beside me, letting my internal peace wash over her like a soothing balm.

Mom often absentmindedly runs her hands through my coat. It's always soft and shiny—one of my great qualities. This time is different. Her fingers are more yearning, like she's creating a tactile memory that she can store for safekeeping. My spirit will remain alive within her as long as my memory remains. There will be times when her insides feel aching and empty, when she longs for my physical presence. My wish is that she fills that emptiness with the memory of my wonderful eyes, the joy and happiness of our time together, the feel of her arms around me.

"I know it's time," she says. "I know you will be okay. I know we will be connected, and I will still be able to talk to you. But... I have a damn big gaping hole in my heart. My head understands—it's just way too much for that beating thing."

She pats her legs like she's just remembered something. A look of recognition crosses her face, and a flicker of light appears in her eyes. She says, "Thank you, thank you, thank you, God, for this body that can feel and sense something so profound, even if it's pain. Thank you for the ability to love someone so totally and unconditionally."

Absolute, true, heartfelt gratitude can heal even the most wounded heart. Mom is going to be okay.

Dad and Dr. Brian are here. It must be two-thirty.

I don't know for sure what just happened. Mom couldn't watch, so I didn't either. A feeling of calm soothing bliss washed over my body. I even jumped into the truck by myself, and I haven't been able to do that for years. Suddenly, all the pain in my body has been swept away.

"Pretty soon, you will only have to think you are somewhere, and there you will be," Mom is saying. But she's looking on the wrong side of the truck seat. If she only hears me and can't see me... oh. I look over and see the old furry body wrapped in a sheet next to me. Thankfully, animals have a more organic understanding of transition. Being separate from my physical self like that doesn't fill me with terror, sadness, or loss. I don't feel any more attachment to that thing than I would an old coat.

Ahhh... and there they are, the colors of transition: red, orange, yellow, green, blue, purple, lavender, and white. It will take about three days for me to pass completely through them. Some call it Crossing the Rainbow Bridge.

Once I pass to the light, my job with my mom will change. Then, you might call me an angel or a guide. We still have more to do, you see.

If you have made it this far, dear reader, please dry any tears. Please join the animal kingdom, the furred, the finned, the feathered or the scaled in the joy and celebration we have in sharing, growing, and learning with you. Please know that by reading our story you have touched all of us.

Forever,

Luke

Author's Note

L uke's story is absolutely true. My supporting cast of beautiful people—Mac, Sharon, and my sweet friends—are also real, and so is almost everyone in this narrative. For legal purposes, when creating the story presence of the less-than-positive people, I changed names, genders, and descriptions, and sometimes I melded two or three people into one character to keep the story uncluttered and increase interest.

Luke truly changed my life and continues to change the lives of thousands of people to this very day.

Page of Gratitude

To Richard Harris for your keen photographer's eye
in artfully capturing the images of Luke. Your time
on this earth was too short. We miss you.

To my editors: Jenipher Mathews, Write My Wrongs Editing,
and Lana McAra, your guidance, knowledge, and talent are
the foundations on which my writer's path will grow.

To Mac, for always supporting my crazy endeavors.
You did sign the release form after all. May we
dance and laugh for the rest of our lives.

To Luke, for choosing me.